CONTENTS

A LIFE BY REQUEST

A walk-in soul's journey from earth to heaven, and back again.
A true story of love, life, and the other side.

Carolyn Jaymes

ISBN: 069287514X
ISBN 13: 9780692875148
Library of Congress Control Number: 2017905466
A Life By Request, East Greenwich, RI

To the love of my lives, present and past, who moved heaven and earth to come back to me. Thank you for being a man on a mission. You are such a gift.

My beautiful children, Tristan and Sam, you mean the world to me. Being your mother has been fun, fulfilling, and I have learned through your eyes so much about life, and myself. Being your mom has been the role of my lifetime. I love you to pieces.

To the incredibly talented spiritual channels who still to this day help me understand the intricacies of the spirit world, thank you for putting up with my constant questions and exploration: April Sheerin, Dr. Meredith, Jackie Eaton, Heather Thor, Lisa Ashton, and Alex in Sedona.

Mom, I know we have had a bumpy road, and I know that you did the best you could. Perhaps we'll try again in another lifetime.

Tom, I truly hope you are now content, fulfilled and at peace with yourself and the decisions you made. I wish you nothing but joy.

My wonderful friends, who still love me even through a story that was tough to believe in the beginning, thank you for not locking me up in that rubber room: Melissa Beliveau, Katie Blessing, Linda MacDonald, Laura Anthony, Alex Champagne, Jessica Kelley and Julie Blackburn.

To my spirit guides, angels and family on the other side, thank you for guiding, directing and offering help along the way. Your support and love has made all the difference: my beautiful and elegant grandmother Johanna, Aunt Gertrude, Jeremiah, Jay's spirit guides - Jim and Joe, Uncle Jerr, and Daddy. To the Grand Council members in the Oatmeal Robes, it has been an honor.

My guides and angels who have not yet officially introduced themselves to me, I know you are there, watching and guiding day in and day out. For that I am eternally grateful.

And to all the people who were with me along the journey, no matter how briefly our paths may have intertwined, thank you for touching my life.

INTRODUCTION

Thank you for joining me on this journey.

This story happened and is still happening to me. I was hesitant about writing this book initially—a reluctant author, you might say. Although people urged me to tell my story, I argued with myself that I would be locked up in a rubber room if I were to explain that the love of my life, who died twenty years ago, asked permission to come back to earth and change places with my husband as a spiritual walk-in. After all, that sounds like the stuff science fiction is made of, doesn't it? I certainly thought so.

In the beginning, I didn't believe any of this walk-in experience. I found no concrete proof that such a thing could take place, no black-and-white science. It was a nice idea, but I found it hard to withhold judgment. As the months and years passed, I slowly began to trust and understand the undeniable truth of what was happening. Once I began to open up to my circumstances, my life changed in a big and wonderful way.

I have now come to understand how important it is for me to share this journey. Despite my initial disbelief that something so incredible was happening to me—or could happen to anyone, for that matter—as the story unfolded and the clues became obvious, I began to believe.

This could happen to anyone, anywhere. And as fate would have it, it happened to me. For those that think miracles and amazing things happen only to other people—smarter, richer, prettier, or, I guess, just special people—I'm here as living proof it's not true. Miracles and manifestations happen everywhere and with anyone. Even me, an average woman from a small New England town.

As I share this story with you, I will do my best to be open and candid, express my true feelings, and share what I have learned about the spirit side and how things work, as far as I understand. What I have striven to offer you is my true, authentic, and down-to-earth story, which I will tell in an informal way—as it occurred. I will share with you how the walk-in progression worked in my situation, how it made a bit of history on the spirit side, and even some of the things we were fortunate enough to learn.

I offer insight into the thoughts, experiences, emotions, and perspectives from the physical, earthbound side as well as the spirit side—an inside look as to why some things transpired as they did, if you will, and how it felt at the time, the viewpoints, the ideas, the joy, and the frustrations. Parts of this book are verbatim from recordings I made while working with a myriad of very talented and gifted people. The rest is my recollection of how things happened along the way—and snippets from my personal journal to fill in some of the blanks.

All names, except for Jay, are changed to protect the identity of individuals and to respect their privacy.

My journey is not yet complete and is still unfolding to this day. This is my interpretation of a story that is true to me. It is my personal experience, my life story, and my love story. Call me crazy, but I'm sticking to it.

Welcome to my little piece of the universe.

1

FIRST READING

"I have a man here to see you, tall, with dark hair, dark eyes," April began.

"Is it my husband?" I asked. My husband, Tom, had brown hair, quickly turning gray, and brown eyes.

"No, not your husband, but close to you. He's coming in heart to heart, which means there is a love connection between the two of you. It's a very strong feeling," April said.

I had no clue who it could have been, so I just kept my mouth shut while she continued.

"Carolyn, do you know what a walk-in is?" April asked me.

"I have no clue," I said to her softly, watching her intently.

"This gentleman is here from the spirit side, and he is standing right next to you. He is very, very upset at how unhappy you are. He knows you are not living the life you agreed to. You are not living the life you were meant to. This is not how things are supposed to be," April said. "He knows you deserve better than this and has been searching for a way to make you happy."

"Really? What a beautiful thought," I replied skeptically. I hadn't been to see a medium for many years and didn't know what to expect. But it certainly wasn't this.

"He's been around you from the spirit side, and he is frustrated by what he's seeing. He said it hurts his heart, watching what you are going through. He knows you don't deserve the unhappiness you have in your life. He wants to come back to you, make your life better." She went on. "He wants to be with you again."

"What the hell?" I was thinking. I didn't know what or whom she was talking about. My brain couldn't understand how this could be, yet there was something about it that touched my heart, and I was open to it.

"I can't express all the feelings he's bringing me. I can tell how much he misses you and how much he loves you. It's overwhelming me, how intense his emotions are with this," April said, looking at me almost in disbelief to get her point across. "He is telling me that he was the love of your life and you were the love of his life."

In an instant I knew who it was; it hit me like a bolt of lightning. It was Jay. I asked April, "Could this be Jay?"

I was met with a serious look from April. "He's saying, 'Yes, could it be any other?' He seems to be bigger than life and has quite a personality. I can tell he's being a bit of a smartass," April said, chuckling. "He's beaming. He is happy you acknowledged him."

She paused, deep in communication with the spirit side. I waited silently, my mind whirling.

"He just leaned down and kissed you on top of the head," she told me.

"Aww, that's so sweet," I said. It was a nice thought, but I didn't feel a thing. "So how can this be? Can he really come back to me?" I asked, hopefully.

"Yes, that is what a walk-in is," she replied. "It is when a new soul enters the body as another leaves and goes back to spirit form. Your soul enters your body when you are born, but with a walk-in it happens between two people. Both parties have to agree to the transfer."

"Really? That's fascinating," I said, wanting to learn more but a little afraid to.

"He seems very serious." She paused again, eyes searching. "Is this making any sense to you?" she asked. I think she was as dumbfounded as I was, trying to understand what was happening.

"Sort of..." I replied, thinking this was probably the strangest conversation I had ever had. "Jay was my one true love, and he died when I was in my thirties."

"He's asking your permission to do this. To come back from the spirit side and be with you," April said.

"What?" I asked in disbelief. "My permission?"

"I'm finding out more..." April said with a faraway look, and after a moment or two, she continued. "From what I understand that he is telling me, he has to go to your husband's soul to ask permission to switch places with him, and he needs to know you are okay with that. So he needs your permission. He's witnessed from the other side how miserable and angry your husband appears to be, and feels he may just agree to a switch." April paused. "He's saying, 'I want things to change for her. I want things to be better. I want her to be happy.'" She looked at me intensely.

This was incredible. It was so hard for me to wrap my head around this, yet my heart leaped at the idea that my life could be different and I could have the love of my life back. "Well, if it really is possible, I openly give my permission." Then I stopped to think of the love I had shared with Jay. It had been a wonderful and special relationship until life got in the way. If he wanted to come back to me, I would welcome him, but that was a big if.

I had no idea how any of it would happen. Or whether it actually could. But if it did, my life would never be the same. Which would be fine with me.

2

MEDIEVAL MANOR, SOUTH BOSTON, MASSACHUSETTS, 1980

Standing in the corridor, waiting to get into the show with a crowd of other guests, Steve, Denise, Kathy, and I were all excited, and a little tipsy. The atmosphere was electric with anticipation and fun as a tall cloaked gentleman walked into the corridor and announced, "Welcome to the Medieval Manor! Are you all ready to greet the king?" We laughed and answered with a resounding "Yes!" perhaps with a little bit more excitement than was called for—but since the ride up to Boston from Rhode Island had been a drinkfest of Rolling Rock and Tango, we were liquored up and raring to go.

The man in the cloak gave us the ground rules. "Number one!" he announced. "You must do what the king says." There were happy murmurings from the group. "Number two!" he bellowed. "There will be absolutely no handling of the wenches!" Lots of snickering and laughter at that one. "Keep your hands to yourself, gentlemen!" he said with a wicked smile while wagging his finger at the crowd. "And number three: if you have to visit the restroom, it is called Canterbury, and you must ask the king for permission to visit Canterbury." It was this last rule that had me worried. With my bladder being the size of a green grape, it wouldn't be long before I had to raise my hand like a little kid in school to relieve myself.

The man in the cloak opened the doors and announced, "The king is holding court in the castle and invites you in for a feast and merrymaking. Long live the king!"

"Long live the king!" we all shouted back, and we entered the banquet room, happy and antsy to continue with the fun, sitting at the communal tables laden with flagons of beer and mead, long loaves of bread, and slices of cheese.

The beer flowed as we all heartily pulled apart the bread with our hands, topped it with chunks of cheese, and began to watch the show. The court jester came out to tell us a few jokes and announce the arrival of the king. When he appeared, to cheers from the crowd, I noticed he was tall, with dark hair and dark eyes, and had an incredible deep voice as he began speaking to welcome us all.

This was followed by the oaf and wenches, who regaled us with song as we continued our feast. Then came the salad, which we ate with our fingers, dipping it in dressing served on the side. I have to admit: having been raised in a stuffy WASP family, I thought this really felt good! I cherished this feeling of being "uncouth," as my father would say jokingly.

While we were eating, there were wonderful actors and singers playing their parts as the king's court, picking people out of the audience to harass, make fun of, and generally give a hard time. This is what people came here for—to let loose, and of course, to eat their dinner with their fingers.

And then, before I knew it, I was wiggling in my seat, pretending that I didn't have to go—but I did. So between the salad and Cornish hen course, I raised my hand. Kathy giggled and pointed at me, Steve just shook his head, and Denise stood up and yelled excitedly while jumping up and down, "Hey, King, over here, over here—she has to go to Canterbury!" I was ready to crawl under my chair at the spectacle, but the feeling of needing to relieve myself was far more demanding, and there was no going back.

The king looked over at me. He wore a devilish grin and crooked his finger, as if to say, "Come here." The crowd laughed and looked around to see who the latest victim would be.

"Okay, here goes..." I thought, and I walked through the long tables of people partying, most eyes on me, looking to see what embarrassment I was going to be subjected to.

As I walked up on the stage, I noticed the king was wearing long deep-purple cloak, a jeweled crown, and thick neck chains, and as I got closer, I noticed he was wearing lots of makeup. He looked at me and said in a loud voice for the audience to hear, "What is your name, m'lady?" Simple question, but there was a look of mischief in his eyes.

"Carolyn," I said.

"Lovely name," he said. "And what would m'lady wish to ask of the king this evening?"

"I have to go to Canterbury," I said, looking at him with a sheepish grin.

He turned his attention to the audience and announced loudly, "It seems Lady Carolyn has to visit Canterbury. What penance should we make her pay for this?"

There were ideas thrown from the audience as someone shouted, "Make her walk the plank!" Another said, "See how long she can wait!" Someone from the back of the room yelled, "To the dungeon with her!" Finally, a young man screamed, "Make her take her shirt off!" The men in the room seemed to love that last suggestion. I wasn't particularly fond of any of the ideas.

"Ah," said the king, "let's ask her to entertain us." The king turned me around to face the audience and continued. "Perhaps you can sing for us. The children's ditty 'I'm a Little Teapot' comes to mind."

"I'm a really bad singer," I said quietly to the king and then added, "And I don't know that song." I was embarrassed to admit that I didn't know such a standard kids' tune, which made sense since I had far from an ordinary "happy" childhood.

"Well, let me see if I can help you," the king offered. He turned me around to face the audience as he placed one of my hands on my waist and gently outstretched my other arm, bending my hand upward to act as the spout. "Okay, sing it together with me—I'm a little teapot, short and stout. Here is my handle; here is my spout. When I get all steamed up, then I shout, so tip me over and pour me out!"

The audience sang along and clapped, between noshing on the food and drinking the libations in front of them. I was just embarrassed. And I really had to go to the bathroom.

When we were through and the clapping and singing died down, the king turned me back to face him, took my hand, and brought it up to his lips. He looked deeply into my eyes, and just before he kissed my hand, he asked, "How does the king find out m'lady's phone number?" I was thinking about how funny that sounded—"king," "m'lady," and "phone number" in the same sentence.

I pulled my hand away gently but firmly. As I did, I looked at him and said with my own version of a devilish grin, "You're the king. You can figure it out." He stared into my eyes and gave me a knowing look, as if he was ready to take on the challenge and would enjoy doing so. I started to pull away. I had to get off that stage. I needed to pee.

I did an about-face and walked off the stage. As I did, he followed me with his eyes and remarked into the microphone he held, "Mmm, yes, very nice indeed. She's a feisty one."

The rest of the night was a great time with my friends. I caught the king looking at me on and off throughout the evening from the stage, and our eyes met many times. The flirting was fun, and I loved the attention.

When the festivities and frolicking were over, we piled back into our cars and headed toward home. "That king certainly had his eye on you all night," Denise said to me.

"I know!" I said. "It was kind of fun."

"Did you give him your number?" she asked me.

"No," I said and told them what had happened between the king and me on stage.

Kathy laughed and said, "Good girl! Make him work for you!"

"Yep," I said, smiling, pleased with myself, but secretly wondering whether I should have given him my number after all. He was kind of cute.

3

MEET THE KING

While I was in college studying to be a chef, I worked for a bank as a teller to help pay the bills and keep me in gas and beer money. It was a job for which I was ill suited. I gave it everything I had, but two things became apparent to me very early on: (1) I was not a numbers person, and (2) I was bored out of my mind with the work. I needed the job, and the customers liked me because I was outgoing and friendly, but my boss didn't think too much of me on the job front, and I definitely caused her some grief. The simple truth was that aside from customer service, I was terrible at my job. I hardly ever balanced my daily teller drawer, and I was forever trying to find the dollar or twenty-five cents that was missing. Once I lost around $800. That was not a good day.

Computers were just beginning to be introduced into banking, and that was another thing that had me stumped. I knew what I was trying to do on this contraption; why didn't it understand what I wanted? Man versus machine at its most basic. We were not friends from the beginning.

Around ten in the morning, the phone rang, and my supervisor, Lisa, answered it. "Carolyn—call for you," she said, looking at me with a sneer. Personal calls at work were frowned on, and I didn't need the distraction.

I picked up the phone and said, "Hi, this is Carolyn."

That velvety voice from the evening before said, "Hello, I believe we met last night. This is the king."

My heart skipped a beat as I said, "Oh, yes. Hello."

"Hello," he said. "I'm Jay."

"It's nice to meet you, Jay," I said as I thought about how much I loved the sound of his voice. "By the way, how did you get my number? I wasn't very helpful to you last night."

"No, but I like a challenge and made it my mission to find out," he said lightly.

"So a man on a mission?" I replied, flirting.

"A man on a mission," he replied. "You made the reservations, and I looked up the number you gave to make them, called your home, and spoke to your mother," Jay reported.

"I see," I said with a sick feeling in the pit of my stomach, hoping she wasn't too hungover.

"And after I explained who I was, she gave me your number at work," he continued.

I wasn't sure whether to be flattered or freaked out. So I just giggled nervously, something I always do when I'm stressed out or overwhelmed.

"It's nice to meet you," the strong, velvety voice said.

"Same here," I replied. "We had a great time at the show last night. It was fun, and you all were wonderful onstage!"

"Glad to hear it," he replied. "Who were you there with?"

"A few friends of mine," I replied.

"So no one special?" he asked.

"My friends are very special to me," I said, playing with him.

"I'm sure they are," he said. I knew Jay was trying to find out whether I had a boyfriend or fiancé or was otherwise taken.

"But if you are asking if I am involved with anyone, the answer would be no, not right now."

"Glad to hear that too," he replied. "I'd love to meet you properly. Perhaps we can get together this week," he said. He wasn't one bit nervous.

"Okay. Sounds like fun," I replied. I felt like a schoolgirl talking to this man, who was seemingly older and worldlier than I was. I thought, chuckling to myself, it must have been my singing that caught his attention.

The evening of our date came, and I was driving toward the milk store in South Attleboro, where I was going to meet Jay. It was near a house I rented with my friends Karen and Patty. I was wondering what kind of evening this was going to turn out to be. Jay was not at all like most men I dated.

As I pulled into the parking lot, Jay was waiting for me, leaning against his old and somewhat-dilapidated powder-blue Chrysler. He was holding flowers for me. "Oh, how sweet!" I thought. I pulled up next to him, and I got out of the car.

"It's very nice to see you again, Carolyn," he said and handed me a little bouquet from the convenience store. "These are for you."

I said, "Thank you," and smelled the flowers, smiling at him.

"Where would you like to go?" he asked while giving me a peck on the cheek. It felt natural.

I replied, "Let's go out for a drink, maybe a bite to eat." Standard line for me.

"Sure," he said. "Hop in. I'll drive."

"No, that's okay. I'll drive. I know the way," I replied. I don't know whether I offered to drive to control the evening, but now, looking back at that moment, I realize what a fool I was because I didn't want to be in his car. It was the eighties, and things like nice cars and expensive toys were far too important to a person's identity. At least to me—someone with such an incredible "I'm not worth it" complex. I needed new and shiny material things to make myself feel as if I was somewhat worthy to be roaming around the planet.

He climbed into my little car, a new Renault 18i—talk about a stupid move on the car-buying front.

He was easygoing and climbed in gingerly, all six feet one of him. He seemed so different from the men I was used to. He seemed calm, kind, and caring, and I thought he might have been a little stoned. At that point—or any other in my life—I was not into drugs. I didn't like to smoke pot, because when I did, I felt out of control and did nothing but eat. And as I was a chubby kid most of my life, that was the last thing I needed. I didn't like coke, because I had friends whose teeth were falling out from snorting too much, and I never understood the appeal. I loved my sleep; I didn't need anything to keep me up facing my life each day. And for the hard stuff, I hated the thought of putting needles anywhere in my body, so no go there either.

Jay stuffed some pot into a small pipe and offered it to me. "No, thanks," I said. He shrugged his shoulders, a gesture I took to mean "fair enough," and put it back into his pocket. Off we went to My Brothers Pub, one of my favorite local hangouts. We ordered a couple of appetizers. I had a stinger, and he had a glass of wine.

We talked about our lives. I wanted to know what it was like to be an actor—I was so intrigued with the idea of being able to be someone else for a living.

After a couple of hours, we drove around, and I showed him some of the places near where I lived. As the night wound down, we headed back to my house, where I knew we would be alone and my roommates, Patty and Karen, would be at work or out for the evening.

We sat down on the daybed used as a couch in the living room, and I turned on the TV. When I sat back down, Jay kissed me, and we immediately started to make out. He was an incredible kisser. I was amazed at how much I enjoyed kissing this man. I was completely caught up. It was a desire I had never felt before. As his lips moved over mine, I couldn't get enough of him. He held me close and pressed his body close to mine as his tongue explored my mouth gently, yet passionately. It was heaven.

After this went on for a little while, I surprised myself by asking, "Do you want to go into my bedroom?" This question was not at all like me. I wanted men to pursue me so I could keep up the good-girl front for as long as I could.

"Are you sure?" he asked, looking into my eyes. Looking back, I could see kindness, gentleness, and desire.

"Yes, I'm sure," I said in a strained voice. We got up from the daybed and moved into my room, just around the corner on the first floor.

I was thinking that I couldn't get enough of this man and wondering why I was acting this way. I am usually a buttoned-up little girl, but I could not wait to get this man into bed. It all seemed so right—not sordid, not too forward, just right.

As we lay on my twin bed, he raised my shirt and took it off over my head. I reached down, and after fumbling for a bit, I unbuckled his belt. He moaned softly. "Mmm."

Taking his time, and between passionate kisses, he slid off the bed, unzipped my skirt, and wiggled it down off my hips and onto the floor. He looked down at me and smiled, making a light growling noise, like an animal about to devour his prey.

I could not wait to get him inside of me. This passion I felt was so strong, almost animalistic. I put my arms out to him to join me on the bed. He lowered himself next to me as we continued to kiss deeply. I groaned as he climbed on top of me. Before we could become one, he climaxed.

"I'm sorry," he said. "Are you disappointed?"

I was so caught up in the moment I didn't even realize what had happened. I didn't want to stop. Now I was the one on the mission. I wanted his hands to keep exploring. "No, it's okay..." I said gently.

"It's been a while since I've made love with anyone," he said, a bit embarrassed.

"Don't worry about it," I said to him. I thought it was so sweet that he didn't want to disappoint me. But I was also crazy with passion and wanted more of him, and quickly.

He realized I needed a release, and I could tell that he wanted to satisfy me, and he went to work to do just that. He knew his way around a woman's body and exactly how to please me. He explored my body and covered me with passionate and light fluttering kisses, deftly concentrating on places that sent me out of my mind. Just when I thought I couldn't stand it anymore, I exploded with a release like nothing I had ever felt before. It felt as if I were transported to another place, outside time and space. This was a release not just of the body but also of the spirit.

"I didn't know it could be that amazing, that anything could feel like that," I said, looking deeply into his eyes and smiling after I caught my breath and settled into his arms.

"Happy?" he said to me after we both caught our breath.

"Oh, yes, very," I said back to him. "You?"

"Yes." He said and held me closer. "I thought I was going to lose you there for a minute..."

"That was incredible, Jay..." I said gently. It was the first time I had called him by his name; it felt good, easy.

"Yes, I got the feeling you liked it," he said and kissed me gently on the nose. I curled up in his arms and fell asleep. This man was beautiful to me in so many ways.

This was not the last time I was going to see Jay. I was hooked, mind, body, and soul.

4

DEALING WITH PARENTS

"How was your date with the king?" my mother asked after I answered the phone the next day. She thought she was being funny, and was trying to bond with me. After what Jay and I had shared together, the question bothered me. He wasn't "the king." He was Jay—a real, honest, and very sexy man I wanted to get to know better. Much better.

I looked at my watch, wondering whether it was after four, the time my mother started her daily bourbon binge. It was safe; she was still sober, as it was only three thirty. I could still communicate with her with some normalcy.

"It was nice," I said. "We went to My Brother's Pub and had a bite to eat and a drink."

My mother thought the whole idea of what Jay had gone through to find me was romantic. She had so little happiness in her own life— a way of living she created for herself. She wanted details.

"That's nice," she replied. "What did you say his last name was?"

"Okay. Here we go with the judgments," I thought. My mother was a racist and a bigot and judged pretty much everyone and everything. Last names mattered to her—it was another way for her to judge people, size them up in her little world, and decide whether they were the kind of people she should associate with. It was insane. It drove me out of my mind and pissed me off completely every time I heard or saw her show her true colors.

My mother wanted to marry me off to the right boy, from the right family, from the right town, who had the right job. Jay would not be that perfect man in her estimation. All the men—well, actually boys, in most cases—that I dated that were a good match for me in her eyes were a complete disaster in mine.

"I didn't," I said. What I felt with Jay was so pure and so special that I was not going to let her cast negativity anywhere near it. I wanted to keep it all to myself for a while. "Sorry, Mom, I have to get back to work," I said, starting to hang up the phone.

"You know, I have some free passes to the exercise studio if you would like them. If you were just a bit thinner, you would be so much more attractive," she said before I hung up.

"Ugh. So you've told me for the last twenty years!" I thought to myself as I sighed lightly. "Good-bye, Mother," I said curtly. "She can be such a bitch," I mumbled under my breath as I hung up the phone, still hoping that someday we could have a normal relationship.

5

FINALLY, SOMETHING I'M GOOD AT!

It turned out that my job at the bank was not a complete loss. During my short tenure, one of the regional directors of the bank wanted to throw a small party for customers opening new 401(k) loans. His name was Rob Burke, and he knew I was in culinary school, and was kind enough to ask me to cater it for him.

I asked him what he would like on the menu, and he asked me to surprise him. Those words were music to my ears; I was in charge, I was in control, and I could prove that I was great at this. Or not.

"Oh, great. Thank you, Mr. Burke," I replied. "I will not let you down!"

The menu for this little gathering of about forty included spinach terrine wrapped and baked in prosciutto, layered with fresh spinach cooked in olive oil and roasted garlic, Boursin cheese, and lightly sautéed slivered almonds, layered between sharp provolone to keep them together while baking. It was served with homemade olive oil and rosemary crostini made from bread I had baked from scratch.

I prepared small finger sandwiches with chunks of chicken breast baked in crème fraiche and tossed with fresh tarragon, aioli, bits of red grapes, and coarse salt. We also had a crudité platter, which was lightly blanched so the colors of the vegetables popped and the vegetables stayed crisp. The crudités were served with a roasted red pepper dip also prepared from scratch.

Also offered were marinated artichoke hearts combined with soft herbed cheese encased in bite-size puff-pastry squares that took me two days to make.

I rented wine glasses and set them up on a separate table with a selection of California wines.

For dessert, I baked a rich, moist carrot cake studded with coconut, walnuts, and pineapple chunks and slathered with fluffy cream cheese frosting.

Everything was fresh, nothing out of a box. It was the only way I cooked. It took time but was so worth it. I was proud of what I had created, and appreciated the fact that Mr. Burke had allowed me to choose the menu.

I think I made about $320 for that gig, and to me it was completely worth it. This was what got me on the road to a career I could sink my teeth into—literally—to find my passion. I adored the creativity and the freedom, and I found out I was good at it.

After the gathering ended, Mr. Burke said as he was leaving, "I'll get a check cut for you for the party tonight, and I'll stop by the bank around eleven tomorrow morning to give it to you."

"Yes, perfect," I said. What I thought was, "I'm in trouble. He didn't like it. He wants to let me down easy." This was where my mind always went. It wasn't good enough. I wasn't good enough.

The next morning at work, Mr. Burke came to me and said, "Here you go," handing me an envelope with the bank logo in the top left corner. "We only have one problem."

"Oh, no," I thought. "What did I do wrong? They didn't like the food, someone got sick, or I didn't clean up well enough." My mind was rambling.

I was instantly brought back to the conversation when I heard Mr. Burke say, "You didn't charge enough."

I looked at him, and my eyes widened. He was smiling.

"Carolyn, you obviously know what you're doing when it comes to food, and I think you may have a great talent. But unless you charge more for your time and work, you will never make it."

"Okay, I get it. That makes sense," I said. "Words of a true banker," I thought. Actually, the amount of money to charge for the evening was hard for me to calculate. I just loved putting it together, and the money was the last thing I was thinking about; it was a pesky detail to me. I loved the creative process and the designing, planning, cooking, and serving of the event menus. I especially loved shopping at the farmers' market in downtown Providence to pick everything out. There was nothing better than getting out of bed at the crack of dawn to take part in the hustle and bustle of the market and pick out exactly what produce I wanted. I loved it all. But figuring out how much to charge was hard—just as hard as trying to balance my drawer as a teller. Numbers were not my thing, and I didn't know my own value, which didn't help much either.

"The food was incredible. It rivaled any restaurant in Rhode Island. And you did it off premise. A feat all on its own," Mr. Burke continued.

I couldn't believe he was saying such nice things. I had no idea that it was that good. I knew it was good, but really, wasn't he going a bit overboard? I thought, blushing, yet thrilled to hear it.

"Thank you so much, Mr. Burke. I'm glad you liked it," I said excitedly. I could tell that he loved the culinary world as much as I did.

"I certainly did," he replied. "As did most everyone else that was here," he said. "Usually we have wine out of a box and cheese cubes, some crackers maybe. But what you did last night was spectacular."

I laughed and nodded my head in agreement. What they had done in the past was pretty pathetic.

"Why don't you make an appointment with my secretary to come and see me? After your hours at the bank, of course. And I will show you an easy way to charge for your services so you can actually make some money," Mr. Burke offered as he handed me his card.

"Thank you very much," I said to him. "I really appreciate it."

"My pleasure," he said as he waved to me and walked out of the branch.

"Wow," I thought. This well-respected man, whom everyone was afraid of in the corporate confines of the bank, was taking me under his wing. Now I was really flying high.

6

THE DATING GAME, BOSTON, 1980

J ay and I were in the car getting ready to head out for the afternoon.

"You've got to help me with a name!" I whined to Jay. He was smart and talented, and in my eyes, he could do anything.

"A name for what?" he asked.

"A name for my catering business!" I replied happily.

"Oh, yes, of course. I'm so glad it went well for you at the bank. So did they love you like I do?" he asked.

"Yes, but certainly not the same way you do," I said, flirting. He smiled and pulled me toward him and gave me a long, deep kiss.

"Not now, Jay. This is serious," I said to him, putting my hand on his chest and gently pushing him away. I was already aroused but refused to give in. "I want to start a real business and need a name! Can you please help me think of one?" He gave up trying to kiss me and pulled away from the curb.

"Great. You should start a business. You're amazing," he said matter-of-factly as we drove off. "But I'm no marketing expert…"

"But you're so creative! You've got to be able to help me think of something. My ideas are all pretty stupid," I replied.

"Okay, I'll think about it. And your ideas are far from stupid. You are very clever, not to mention creative," he said as he lit the small amount of pot in his little pipe and took a puff. "Let's see: a one-woman show, cooking for people in their homes, small parties, great food from scratch, gourmet—what does that word 'gourmet' mean anyway? It's kind of pretentious."

"To me it means that everything is from scratch, natural, best ingredients, creative." We drove around a bit, heading to pick up some groceries to bring back to his apartment.

It took him only a few moments to come up with something. "I've got it!" he blurted out.

"Oh, goody. What?" I said excitedly.

He put his index finger up and said in his most commanding voice, "The Secret Ingredient."

"Perfect! I love it," I said as I wrapped my arms around him in a big hug and planted several little kisses on his face. He veered off the road slightly, looking at me happily as he righted the car.

"I love you!" I said to him. So that was it; I was in business.

We stayed in Jay's apartment after we returned from the store. It was a windy and rainy afternoon. Jay had the night off from work, and we wanted to just stay in and relax.

I wandered into one of his guest bedrooms and found hundreds of *National Geographic* magazines lined up in perfect rows. There were four huge bookcases filled with them, set up by date, going back for years.

"Wow!" I said as I looked back to the couch in the living room, where Jay was still sitting, watching a Boston Celtics game. He loved basketball. "Have you read all these?" I asked.

"Yes," Jay replied. "Every one, cover to cover." He was only half paying attention to me; his eyes were on the game.

I looked at him in amazement. "Unbelievable," I said.

"Not as unbelievable as you," he said as he looked at me from the other room.

I walked back into the living room as Jay watched me closely—the basketball game no longer of any interest to him. He had other things on his mind now. I sat back down on the couch, and he pulled me closer, ignoring the game playing in the background.

He kissed me lightly on the cheek, slowly moving his way down to my earlobe, where he nibbled gently. Jay knew this sent me over the edge. He found out early on in our relationship and had taken advantage of the knowledge ever since. We began kissing deeply as he slipped his hand under my blouse and loosened my bra. As he caressed my breasts, I let my hands wander down over his stomach and began stroking his thighs, making sure I caressed him gently between his legs.

"Let's go into the bedroom," he murmured into my ear as he continued nibbling. The urgency was building.

"How about we stay right here," I replied. I was so comfortable in his arms. I fit there perfectly and didn't want to lose the momentum. We kissed for a few minutes more, exploring each other.

"Mmm, but we would be so much more comfortable..." he said. I knew why he wanted to move to the bedroom: so we could be free from the space restraints of the couch to explore our sexuality with lots of room to experiment.

I stood up, thinking about how much fun this could be, and held out my hand for him to follow me into the bedroom as he suggested; my shirt was still undone. He reached up and caressed my breasts and sat in front of me, covering me in kisses.

"I need to keep them warm," he said softly. He moved downward and began to kiss my stomach while reaching behind me to unbutton my skirt.

I placed my hand over his, looked down at him, and said, "Let's get comfortable."

He looked up at me with his beautiful deep-brown eyes as he was kissing my breasts and I was holding his head to my body. He released his kiss and rose and followed me. We continued to undress each other slowly and passionately, eagerly discovering each other's desires. Jay gently laid me down on the bed, and I lay there with nothing on but a strand of pearls. "Mmm, I love those June Cleaver beads. You are so sexy when it is the only thing you have on," he said with a small growl, looking down at me on the bed.

I pulled his face closer to mine, kissing him deeply, not wanting to wait another minute for the slow, smooth, and expressive lovemaking we had become so good at. "I love your lips, and your voice...they really turn me on," he said as he continued covering my body with kisses.

It was a wonderful afternoon, and after we made love, we slept in each other's arms until we woke up hours later, both completely famished.

Later that night we were sitting in Jay's favorite Chinese restaurant on Route 9. He ordered hot-and-sour soup and lo mein, and I ordered shrimp and peanuts.

We looked at the menus, reading aloud the horoscopes that pertained to the years we were born. We were both rats in the Chinese astrological calendar; Jay was born in 1948, and I in 1960.

Jay said, "Listen to this. It says, 'Ladies belonging to the rat zodiac sign are pretty, smart, and lovely. They have quick minds and dexterous hands and are able to learn anything.'"

I looked at him and giggled like a schoolgirl.

"I especially agree with the dexterous hands..." Jay said with one eyebrow raised.

"Yes, Jay. I know you love my wandering hands," I replied with my best authoritative voice, pretending to act as if he were a pest—which, of course, he wasn't. I loved every minute of it and every inch of him.

"My legs are still twitching," I said to him.

"What do you mean?" he asked.

"My thighs are twitching," I repeated. "Almost like they are vibrating. It's a crazy feeling."

"Between your legs?" Jay questioned.

"Yes," I said, blushing.

"It's your G-spot," he said.

I had no idea what he was talking about. I looked at him quizzically.

"I read about this. While we make love, if I can find your G-spot and spend some time there..." He looked at me with a knowing smile.

"You can have an out-of-the-ordinary experience that can last quite a while."

"Was that what you were trying to do this afternoon?" I asked, thinking back to our lovemaking earlier and how it was certainly out of the ordinary, for me at least.

"Yes, I just want to please you," he said with loving eyes.

"Well, you certainly accomplished that!" I replied with a happy laugh. "I was wondering how you could hold me up that long."

"Man on a mission," he said to me, smiling.

"You're amazing," I replied. We both smiled at each other and turned back to our menus.

7

GETTING THE MENU STRAIGHT

"We would like participative hors d'oeuvres again," Joan said to me as we sat in her office in the ivory towers of the bank. The irony of the situation was not lost on me. This woman had worked in the branch I started in and tried to fire me for not balancing my teller drawer. I probably did deserve to be fired, but I was saved by Rob Burke and my cooking skills. My little business had come a long way. Not only was I being hired by all sections of the bank, right up to the office of the president, but the word spread, and soon enough I was catering events for rock bands, politicians, some large corporations, weddings, and so on. We were busy, and it was exciting.

I left the bank just a couple of months after my first catering gig. Mr. Burke came to me at the time and told me that if I needed to decide about my future, he suggested I let the bank go and concentrate on cooking. He was saying to me in a nice way to get out before I got fired, and I got the message—although I did need to work and make money so I could get back out of the craziness of my parents' house, where I was living again. The house I was renting with Karen and Patty in South Attleboro was being sold, and I was hard pressed to find another place at the right price, so back home I went.

I laughed. "Yes, you guys definitely like the participative hors d'oeuvres!" We were talking about some of the passed appetizers for which there was something the guests had to do: dip something, cook something, put something together, or pierce something with a small fork.

Joan flipped through the catering brochure and pointed out a few things that she thought would be good. "Sesame Dijon chicken," she said. "Everyone always loves that."

"Okay," I said, writing it down in my notebook.

"Oh, and the prosciutto and portabella mushroom in puff pastry too," Joan said. "Also the grilled swordfish in lemon crème skewers."

"Great, those are always a big hit," I said, thinking to myself that yet another batch of puff pastry had to be made from scratch. It was a lot of work, but worth it.

"Oh, just put together something wonderful!" Joan said as she looked at her watch. "I have someone waiting for me in the lobby." Joan began to walk away and added, "Please don't forget the crudité and charcuterie platters too. I love your spinach terrine."

"Happy to. I'll get a proposal over to you by the end of the week," I said to her.

"Great, I'll talk with you later," Joan replied.

I entered the beautiful lobby and pressed the button for the private elevator. The elevator doors opened, and there before me was the president of the bank, a woman I really admired. When she was appointed as bank president, she was one of the first woman in the Northeast in that position.

"Hello, Carolyn," she said. "I'm glad I ran into you."

"Nice to see you, Mrs. Santine," I replied.

"It seems congratulations are in order," she said.

"Oh, thank you, but what for?" I said, not knowing what she was talking about.

"You must not have read the paper this morning," she said to me.

"No, I didn't have a chance yet. What did I miss?" I said, my interest piqued. I had had trouble sleeping the night before because I could hear my mother in her routine drunken stupor clamoring around the house. We lived in a small ranch, and my bedroom was just off the kitchen. Most of the night, I would hear her fumbling for ice to make herself drinks. Later, she would graduate to the knife drawer and fumble around for a knife. I never knew whether she was looking for a knife to kill herself or me. But I always felt it was me. I was typically wide eyed in my bed until she finally stumbled down the hallway, falling into the walls and closet doors with a bang, and then flopped into bed. When the ritual was over, I could finally sleep.

I shook my head to erase the memories of the night before and heard Mrs. Santine go on to say, "You have been awarded the Rhode Island Business Woman of the Year Award! There was a blurb about it in the business news section. It seems you will be honored at an event with women from each state who also won."

"Really? Wow, that's wonderful!" I replied. "Thanks for letting me know!" I was so busy and had ignored some phone calls I probably should have returned, which was why I didn't know about the award. I had been interviewed by the US Small Business Administration a couple of times because of my growth in the business and my young age. By this point I had been in the local newspaper and business magazines and had been asked to do TV and radio interviews. I enjoyed it.

"It's great to see women succeed in business. Keep it up. You're making us look good!" she said, smiling.

"Thank you very much, Mrs. Santine. You are a wonderful role model."

She smiled warmly and touched me on the arm as the elevator doors opened and she walked out.

I stood in the elevator beaming to myself. "Wow," I said to myself. "How cool."

8

CAN'T GET ENOUGH

It was late in the morning, and Jay and I were standing in the kitchen of his third-floor walk-up apartment in Waltham. I was rummaging around the refrigerator, looking for the ingredients to make an egg cream. "Oh, bummer, we don't have any seltzer!" I said.

We had slept in since we had gotten back to his apartment late the night before, after returning from Newport, where we had dinner. It was a beautiful night, and there were huge puffy clouds scattered in the sky, which appeared dark blue against the incredible full moon. As we drove down Ten Mile Drive after dinner, we pulled into a small parking lot reserved for visitors at the lookout spot near a jetty that stretched out into the ocean. We both got out of the car and held hands as we walked toward a wooden bench and sat down, looking out onto the expanse of the Atlantic Ocean. We sat for a few minutes taking in the view. Then Jay put out his hand to help me up, and together we climbed down the rocks toward the ocean. We laughed as we slipped and unsteadily found a flat spot overlooking the sea, waves crashing around us. We could feel the mist on our faces. The setting was incredible.

He turned to me and looked deeply into my eyes. "Do you have any idea how much I love you?" he said.

"I think I do," I said, smiling, with complete love in my eyes. He leaned toward me and kissed me with emotion that seemed to be reserved just for this moment. As the waves crashed around us and the mist rose from the sea, we stood in a comfortable embrace. The moon was full and bright; I could see every beautiful feature of Jay's face. It was the most romantic moment of my life. I knew Jay felt how special it was too. Standing there in each other's arms was beautiful; the feeling was almost palpable. It felt as though we were transported into another place—a blissful, peaceful place where love ruled all.

"I love you so much. I didn't know it was possible to have a love like this," I said, looking up at him.

"Just for you my dear," he said. "Only for you."

We stayed in that perfect spot by the sea exchanging soft, passionate kisses for what seemed like an eternity.

As I was lost in my thoughts of the night before, I heard Jay talking to me.

"I said let's go back to bed. I don't have a show until three," Jay said, coming up behind me and wrapping his arms around me, resting his head on my back. It was a beautiful sunny Sunday morning, and we were both physically spent from a night of incredible passion followed by a great night's sleep.

As I tried to wriggle out of his embrace, he held me closer. "I just want to please you," he whispered as he began nibbling my ear. I could feel the stirring deep in my body, but I just didn't think I had it in me again.

"I know, and I love you for it, but I've got to get home. And besides, you pleased me three times last night, Jay. Isn't that enough?" I was spent. And hungry.

"Last night was pretty special, wasn't it?" he said to me as he kissed the back of my neck and stepped away from me so I could get on with making our ritual after-sex egg creams. Jay had them as a boy growing up in Brooklyn and showed me how to make them "the right way." I loved having a peek into his childhood.

I turned to him and said quietly, "Yes, very special."

"And I don't just mean the lovemaking," he continued. "Just being with you there on the rocks was so sensual."

"It was beautiful, and so romantic." I looked at him. "I love you."

Jay came over to me and kissed me on the top of my head. "How are those egg creams coming?"

Jay and I had been dating for many months, and I was falling in love with him, hard. He made me feel good, and I knew he loved me. I decided it was time to ask him. "I was thinking maybe you would like to meet my parents sometime," I said nervously.

"I can do that," Jay replied. I knew what he was thinking—he had asked me a couple of times whether I would like him to meet them, but I was afraid. Jay was twelve years older than I, an actor, and Jewish. None of these things were of consequence to me, but to my little WASP family, especially my mother, it was out of the ordinary, and unacceptable in her eyes. I couldn't have cared less about what she thought about this; what worried me was how it would affect Jay. I really didn't want to expose him to my family, and I was afraid of what he would think of them. Would he stop loving me when he met my parents? I knew he never would think that way. It was time to take the relationship one step further.

Both my parents were alcoholics. My mother was also a bigot and a racist. I was so ashamed of her for it. My father, on the other hand, was open and caring, forward thinking, and had a great outlook on life. He always told me that he believed that people were basically nice and wanted to be kind. Thank heaven for my father. He was at least one bit of sanity in my life. But he drank because he was unhappy. My mother drank because she was depressed. They never drank together to celebrate or have fun. They drank to get drunk, day in and day out.

It was why I kept people away and almost never had friends over. Only when I was very sure of myself or the kindness of the other person would I bring anyone into the house. I didn't want to subject them to the drunken stupor my parents were in on a daily basis. I was stuck with it, but I didn't want to subject others to it. They didn't deserve it.

"Okay, great. I will set it up. Maybe next Sunday, if you don't have to work," I said to Jay, silently asking myself whether this was really a good idea after all.

"Sounds good," he replied and then turned me around and gave me a long, deep kiss as we fumbled back toward the bedroom. "Now let's get to more pleasing..." he said as he kicked the bedroom door shut with his foot and we tumbled onto the bed. The egg creams were going to have to wait.

9

DREADED MEETING

"So you're still dating the actor?" my mother said to me. "That's not a very stable job, is it?" She was more concerned about what her sisters and friends would say about the fact I was dating an actor. She didn't care whether I was happy; her concern was how it looked from the outside to everyone else.

I had the day off from work, and it was late in the afternoon, around four thirty. The drinking had begun already. My mother was sitting in her favorite chair, which stank of booze and cigarettes, in the otherwise-lovely family room. I wanted to get this over with and get them all in the same room—let the chips fall where they may.

"Yes, and I think he is wonderful. I thought you might like to meet him," I replied.

"Well, I guess so..." my mother said to me as she took a gulp of bourbon and water from her favorite roly-poly glass. Her drink was typically made up of about three-quarters bourbon and one-quarter water. It started every afternoon at exactly four o'clock, when she would announce, "I'm parched." She pretty much stared at the clock most of the afternoon until it was four o'clock, just so she could begin to slip into her daily oblivion.

"If your father says it's okay," my mother said. I didn't understand where that had come from; she didn't care what my father thought about much of anything. She was in charge.

I asked my father whether he would mind Jay coming over that following Sunday. He was usually up for anything.

"No problem!" he said. Those seemed to be his two favorite words. He never saw a problem with anything. I loved my father very much and did want Jay to meet him. He was a little piece of normal in our otherwise-crazy household.

"Okay, that's settled," my mother said as she took another long sip of her drink.

"Okay, I'll have him come by early afternoon, around one," I said. The last thing I wanted to do was rope Jay into having a meal at my house. That would mean we wouldn't have a quick getaway. And he would have to put up with my mother's cooking, which was dreadful.

It was the following Sunday morning, and Jay drove down from Waltham in his old Chrysler, showing up ten minutes early. I ran out to the car as he approached, and I could see my mother checking out the situation from the window. She looked at his car and then at Jay, and out of the corner of my eye, I could see a look of mild disgust on her face, although she tried to mask it. He had a full beard at this point, which I knew she wouldn't like. I knew she thought he wasn't good enough in general. Not that he wasn't good enough for her daughter, just that he wasn't good enough, period. No rhyme or reason—he just didn't have the right look about him.

As we walked up the short staircase to the family room, I opened the door and ushered Jay into the room. It was filled with smoke, as usual, but the house looked pretty good; it was neat and tidy.

Jay brought one of his little convenience store bouquets of flowers, and as I reached out to take them from him, I could see he had two bundles. He separated them and handed one to my mother and one to me. She was so elated over the little gesture of flowers; it occurred to me how little happiness she had in her life. It was nice to see something brighten her up.

I introduced everyone, and my father shook Jay's hand with warmth. We all shared some small talk, and Jay and my father talked about the Freemasons for a while. My father was a member, and Jay seemed to know the history of the organization and what it stood for. He was amazing; he seemed to know something about everything.

The afternoon was filled with tension for me; I was just waiting for my mother to say something obnoxious about Jay being too old for me or that he didn't have a "real job." But she was well behaved—for a little while, at least.

I thought to myself how ironic it was that my mother thought she was so much better than he because her family had come over on the *Mayflower* or some such nonsense and that another branch of our family had settled one of the islands off the coast of New England. It was such bullshit. What difference did it make? How could that possibly make one person better than another? The thought of it made my blood boil. All I saw in our extended family was phoniness and an appreciation for things that didn't amount to a hill of beans.

Jay was a wonderful man who truly loved me. He was far more educated than my mother, more intelligent than she, kinder, happier, more giving of himself...the list went on and on.

Almost on cue, as I was thinking that very thought, she piped up and said, "So I understand you have a pretty-high IQ."

"Uh-oh," I thought to myself. I willed her to keep her mouth shut, but it didn't work.

Then she went on to ask, "Why would you want to become an actor when you could do just about anything?"

"Here we go..." I thought with a sick feeling in my stomach, wondering how she knew this. Then I remembered Jay and I had been with my cousin Naomi, and they had been discussing their IQs. Naomi must have mentioned the conversation to her mom, who told her sister, my mother. I'm sure the two sisters spent an afternoon talking about this fact over coffee. Gossip was their lives.

I remembered the scene. Naomi, Jay, and I were watching a documentary about how IQ is measured. "Well, my IQ is one thirty-five," Naomi said while taking a drag from her cigarette. Naomi had a way of stating things in an I-know-everything tone. She was also a good friend, and I loved her to pieces.

Jay sat on the couch near her and said, "Mine is one fifty-seven."

I whipped my head around from where I was sitting at the kitchen table playing solitaire. "Really?" I asked, completely taken aback. "Isn't that Einstein territory?"

"Almost," he said with a grin, being neither pompous nor bragging.

Two things went on in my mind at this point. One was that I didn't have a clue as to what my IQ was, but I was sure it wasn't in Einstein territory or anywhere near it. The second thing was "How could a man this intelligent love me?" There it was again, my "I'm not worth it" internal conversation rearing its ugly head.

"Wow, that's high," Naomi said to him as if he didn't already know it. It wasn't often she came across someone as smart as she was, much less with a higher IQ. I think she respected him a little bit more for that. He was on her level now. She liked that, and as someone who felt as though I never measured up to her, so did I.

Jay continued with a chuckle. "Yeah, it was funny how I found out. My mother took me to the shrink when I was thirteen because I spent all my time locked in my room, reading. I never wanted to do anything else. She thought something was wrong with me and was convinced I was crazy. So after three weeks of tests and doctor visits, one night the phone rang." He took a sip of his drink and continued. "My mother answered the phone, and I heard her talking to the doctor. Then she fainted right there on the kitchen floor, leaving the phone dangling!" He started laughing. "My brothers and I picked her up and asked what happened once she came to. She shook her head and said, 'Jay is a genius.' We all looked at one another in disbelief. Everyone was expecting the doctor to say I was nuts."

The three of us were roaring in laughter at this point.

"Yep, and I don't think it made my mother happy one bit when the doctor told her to let me do what I wanted and encourage me in whatever direction my mind took me, follow any path that was of interest to me." He had a huge smile on his face, looking completely proud of himself over this fact as he continued. "She has never forgiven me for becoming an actor. One of my brothers is a social worker, and the other works in the White House, and I'm just the *actor*!"

We all laughed a bit more and shook our heads in disbelief. "Well, this would explain the entire room full of books and *National Geographic*s in your apartment," I said to him.

"Yep," he replied. "I still read everything I can get my hands on."

"Wow," I replied. "You amaze me."

I gently shook my head to bring me back out of the daydream.

"Mom, please!" I pleaded.

"What's the matter? I was just wondering. After all, he could do anything he wanted to do," she argued.

"Yes, and he has chosen to be an actor. So good for him. He's happy," I argued back. At this point I was going to lose control—usually our arguments were not screaming matches but more along the lines of who could be more passive-aggressive. Who could ignore whom more effectively. Who could better wound the other with a smile. She had it mastered, and I was a novice but was learning for sheer survival purposes. But at this point, I was just plain mad.

Jay chimed in. "Performing arts has interested me the most out of everything I have done, so it was the natural path for me to take." He wasn't upset by the question; his answer seemed a bit rehearsed, as if he'd had to answer the question many times before.

I knew what this question was really about. If in fact I were ever to marry this man, it would be acceptable if he were a doctor or a lawyer. "If you need a lawyer, make sure he's Jewish. Jewish lawyers make lots of money," I remember my mother saying more than once. The way her mind worked sometimes made my skin crawl.

It was obvious this was going to be a short visit; she was acting up already. I glanced at Jay. He sat in the chair next to me, petting our dog, Walter. He was serene, calm. None of this was bothering him, and he actually seemed to be enjoying it. I thought to myself how graceful he was to put up with my family so well. Then I wondered whether this family visit would break us up. I doubted it though; he was too open minded for something like that. I had to admit I did really want to know what he thought about my parents.

We lasted for another hour or so, when I had had enough and was more than ready to leave. My mother had gone through half a pack of cigarettes, and I couldn't breathe. My father was well into his eight-beer Sunday regimen. Soon it would be four, when my mother would announce, "I'm parched!" and start on her bourbonfest. Jay had seen enough; I didn't want to push it.

"Well, we've got to leave. Jay and I are going to meet some friends." I was making that up. We were not going to see friends; we were going straight back to his apartment to have sex. Over and over, I hoped. I needed it after this. I thought he did as well, and if he didn't, I knew he would at least welcome the idea.

Jay held my hand as we walked toward the car. I was relieved it was over. I thought for sure this little visit to meet my parents would end in disaster—or him wondering how he could ever get involved in a family like mine.

We waved as we pulled out of our driveway. My mother was looking out the window, checking out the situation. At this point I couldn't have cared less what she thought; I just wanted to get the hell out of there.

As we drove back to Boston, I couldn't wait to ask. "So what do you think?"

"They seem nice..." he said to me as he filled his pipe with the last bit of pot he had in the little plastic bag in his pocket.

"Nice?" I said to him in a deadpan voice. "Nice?"

"Yes, nice," he replied, reaching out and squeezing my hand.

"C'mon, what do you really think?" I was not giving up till I heard some truth, or at least something I wanted to hear.

"Okay, I think they have some strong opinions, but they have the right to think them. And other than that, they really do seem nice. You are a lot like your mother."

My heart sank. "What? How could you say that?" I just about exploded at the thought.

"You both have bubbly personalities, and you are both easy to talk to, outgoing," he said. "And I love your father's laugh. I see where you got it from." I have always had a loud laugh—a jolly, hearty laugh, just like my father. One that, when strangers heard it, would make them either look at me quizzically or giggle and join in.

I was pissed. I had a right to bitch about my mother; she was a bigot, a racist, and an uncaring, demeaning, and judgmental mother. But to compare me to her? That hurt.

"Look," he said, "she's not the best mother to you, but she does have some redeeming qualities, and I see them in her. She will never measure up to the incredible daughter of hers I love so much, but she's not all bad."

"Okay," I said, "ten points scored for Jay." He offered me the pipe, and I took a deep puff. It was time to unwind.

I knew Jay was being kind and open minded. I realized he didn't have the background I had with her, and he was giving her the benefit of the doubt. As we drove up I-95 toward Boston, I thought back to what it was like to be her little girl. When I was small, around three or four, I was happy all the time and wanted to show her how much I loved her. She was relaxing in the living room with a cocktail, drinking bourbon even that far back, and I tried to crawl up to sit on her lap. I was in my little green dress and black patent leather Mary Jane shoes as she pushed me off, her drink sloshing in her glass. She was very annoyed, saying, "Get off of me! You're a haunt!" as she wiped the spilled drink and the remnants of me off her skirt. Now at that age, I didn't know what a haunt was, but I guessed it was pretty bad. I had no idea what I had done, and after trying to climb back up on her lap a few times after that to snuggle, with pretty much the same result, I stopped. The rest of my childhood was about the same, but I never gave up hope that someday she would be glad I was her little girl, and we would be a close family after all.

Thinking back on it now, I see this episode with my mother has haunted me my entire life. Ironic, isn't it? Years later, as I began my spiritual journey, she came back to me through mediumship and apologized for not being the mother I needed. I think she is tormented by that now a little bit. I have forgiven her and hope she can move on.

"I take it your childhood was not a bed of roses," Jay said to me as he reached out and held my hand. He knew my mother and I were not close, but I never filled him in on any of the details. I didn't want him to have to put up with my whining about it. He seemed genuinely interested in why we had this tenuous relationship, or at least why she drove me nuts all the time.

"Yes, but I'm sure most people had issues growing up too," I said.

"My childhood was pretty happy overall," Jay said. "Some usual family stuff, but while we were kids living in Brooklyn, my brothers and I had a good childhood. My mom was very funny and took good care of us. We laughed all the time. We didn't have a lot, but we were happy."

That was nice to hear. "That's wonderful," I said to Jay, truly pleased for him that he had such love and laughter in his childhood home. I could picture him and his two brothers in a little house in Brooklyn, raising havoc and having a great time. I was sure that much of his childhood shaped the wonderful man he had become.

"Do you want to talk to me about it?" he asked. It was clear I was upset about the visit, and he was genuinely interested in hearing more.

"No, not really," I replied. "It's just a simple case of Mummy-doesn't-love-me blues." I was referring to one of my favorite Elton John songs. Jay had surprised me with tickets to see Elton John at the Boston Garden a few weeks earlier. Jay knew he was one of my all-time favorite performers and, as always, just wanted to make me happy.

"Okay, well, if you ever want to talk about it..." Jay said.

"Thanks, honey, I will. I love you," I replied, not sure when that would ever be.

10

ALWAYS WITH THE FLOWERS

We planned to meet at a local pub in Boston on Lansdowne Street. Kenny and Alice, two other actors from Medieval Manor, were going to meet us there; I was looking forward to it. I pulled my little blue car up to the curb, luckily finding a parking space right up front.

I spotted Jay walking toward me with a small bouquet of flowers. Every time we met, he brought me flowers, whether from the local convenience store or from a garden, or roses on special occasions. Either way, he always had a bouquet or single flower for me. I thought it was romantic and loved it.

"You don't have to bring me flowers every time you see me!" I said to him as he approached. I wrapped my arms around him in a big hug.

"You are a beautiful woman, and you deserve them. I like doing it. Besides, I love you," he said.

I gave him a sweet smile, and he gave me a peck on the cheek. We walked into the pub, Jay holding the door for me as we walked in.

We ordered drinks and some appetizers and started talking. "You guys are so much fun!" I said to them. I was used to buttoned-up, snooty country club kids, who were incredibly boring and talked only about cars, themselves, and gossip. Jay's friends were great conversationalists, witty and fun, and so talented. I loved being around them.

Alice, who was one of the wenches at the Manor and a very good friend of Jay's, was interested in photography and studying it at Boston University. "Hey," she began, "I was wondering if you and Jay would sit for me for a photo shoot. We are putting together black-and-white photos for a show. I think you two would be great. You both have such different looks. Carolyn, you are fair skinned and have light hair—"

"And you are gorgeous!" Jay added. I blushed.

"And Jay, with your dark hair and brooding eyes, it would be a great contrast," Alice said as she looked at Jay, then me, then back again.

"Brooding eyes?" Jay said, chuckling lightly. "Huh..."

"Oh, that would be fun!" I said.

"Sure," Jay said. "Anything for you, Alice." Alice was one of Jay's closest friends. It was nice to see the interaction between the two of them; they were like brother and sister.

"Great, so meet me at the studio Wednesday on Comm. Ave. around noon," Alice instructed.

"Do I need to bring anything?" I asked. "Anything special you want us to wear?"

"Just wear dark colors. This is a black-and-white photo shoot, so you should wear black. That would be perfect. And bring a little makeup for last-minute touch-ups."

"Okay," I said. "Sure."

"You don't need makeup," Jay said as he stroked my hand. "You're perfect just as you are, and I wouldn't want you to cover up any of those adorable freckles."

"I love you," I thought to myself as I looked at him with sheer infatuation.

"Ready?" I said to Jay later that week as we were getting ready to meet Alice.

"Yes, I'm glad we're getting professional pictures of you and me. It's nice of Alice to ask us."

"It was nice of her," I replied. "I really like her." Alice was one of those people who were simply kind. She was smart and talented, but what you felt right away upon meeting her was her kindness.

"By the way," Jay said, "the other night at work, Kenny and Alice were talking to me about you."

"Oh?" I said, hoping it wasn't too bad.

"Yes, they told me how much they liked you and that you were a keeper," he said, smiling at me.

"Aww. That's so nice!" Those few words meant the world to me. I was accepted.

After spending close to three hours with Alice, taking pictures, Jay and I said our good-byes and stopped at Faneuil Hall, looking for a place to grab a bite to eat.

"I hope the photos will come out all right," I said.

"Oh, I'm sure they will. Look at what she had to work with," Jay said.

"C'mon," I said. "I'm serious. It's important for Alice. I want to make sure she captured what she needed."

"You are so photogenic, and I'm not too bad myself," he said with a grin. "There wasn't much to do, so I'm sure they will turn out great. Alice seems to know what she's doing."

"Okay, I'll guess we'll see." It wasn't that I thought I would do something wrong; I was just not sure I was pretty enough to be plastered on the gallery walls.

As if he knew exactly what I was thinking, Jay said, "The first time I laid eyes on you, I thought you were the most beautiful woman in the world."

"Mm-hmm," I replied sarcastically.

"No, seriously, that first date we had, when I drove down to see you and we met at the gas station, or milk store, or whatever it is you Rhode Islanders call it? You got out of the car and walked toward me, and I thought, 'She is the most beautiful woman I have ever seen.' You took my breath away. Honestly."

"Yeah, right," I replied, rolling my eyes. It wasn't just a ploy for more compliments. I genuinely didn't believe him.

"I did. And why do you do that anyway?" Jay said, a little annoyed.

"Do what?" I asked.

"Put yourself down so much. You are incredible, not to mention beautiful, inside and out!" He was getting annoyed. I could tell this had been building up for a while.

"Oh, stop it. You are just acting now." I was embarrassed by his words and was not having any of what he was saying. But at the same time, it made me feel good.

This sent him over the edge. "Why do you keep saying that? I don't turn on and turn off acting to suit my needs. I'm not acting when I am with you. This is me!" Jay exploded.

"Okay, okay, sorry!" I replied, putting my hands up in surrender. Sometimes I secretly thought Jay turned on his acting to get me into bed. Sex was almost all he ever thought about. He seemed to be on a constant mission for it. Seeing him so upset by my words, I realized that I was being unfair. It was just me wallowing in my little "I'm not worth it" world.

"I'm sorry. I didn't mean to hurt you." I apologized, and then put my arms around him, and rested my head on his shoulder.

"It's okay. Just know that I love you. Very much," he said to me and kissed the top of my head.

11

BIGGER STAGE

Months later, Naomi and I drove up to Lowell to see Jay in *Talley's Folly* by Lanford Wilson at the Merrimack Repertory Theatre. He was playing the lead role of Matt Freidman, and I was excited to see him on stage. As I sat there in the audience, watching his commanding presence, I realized that he had so much more talent than I ever realized.

"He's good!" Naomi leaned over to me and whispered about thirty minutes into the performance. The play is supposed to be exactly ninety-seven minutes long, and at the beginning, the main character Matt Freidman speaks to the audience directly, explaining that he will try to capture and relate the story in that amount of time. It was fun to watch.

"I know!" I said to Naomi with my eyes wide in agreement. I had never seen Jay in a production like this. Smaller ones in Gloucester and other areas outside of Boston, but this was wonderful to watch. Little did we know that in later years as a walk-in, he would be playing the role of a lifetime—the role of two lifetimes, really.

Later, after the performance, I spotted Jay. "You were great!" I said to him as he came out looking for us after the performance and curtain calls were over and the audience was almost through filing out of the theatre. He had asked me beforehand to wait for him or meet him backstage, but I guess he didn't want to take any chances and so came out right after the performance, in full costume and makeup, to find us and usher us into the party backstage.

"Why, thank you," he said. "I'm glad you both were able to make it."

"Nice job!" Naomi said. "I really enjoyed it."

We both hugged Jay to congratulate him and made our way backstage.

Kenny and Alice had also come to see the performance, and we met them backstage. We all exchanged pleasantries, and everyone gave kudos to Jay for a great performance.

As we were talking, the actor playing Sally, the lead role opposite Jay, came up to him and gave him a big kiss and a hug. I felt a twinge of jealousy but dismissed it. I was being ridiculous. He loved me so much.

As we milled around at the party, many other performers and friends told Jay how great he was, and he reciprocated where he could. It was great to see how tight this group was; they all truly seemed to like one another and appreciate one another's talent.

"Your friends love you," I said to Jay.

"My fan club," he said and laughed softly.

"You can make fun if you want, but I thought you were wonderful, and from what I can see, so did everyone else," I said to him.

"Well, thank you. One of these days I have to get out to California. That's where the really good parts are," he replied.

My imagination immediately went to us moving to California, him getting all the great parts he wanted, me playing house and raising a family.

Later at the party, I asked Kenny about it. "If anyone has the talent to make it, it's Jay," he said. "We all know it. But he doesn't seem to be able to pull the trigger and go!" Jay was starting to land a few commercials and small recurring parts in a series filmed in Boston, but the work he really wanted was on the West Coast.

Later that night, as we lay in bed, I asked Jay, "Do you really want to go to the West Coast?"

"I'm thinking about it," he said. "It only makes sense if I want to continue to grow as an actor. I'm a little stuck where I am here in Boston."

"Well, you need to do whatever it is that makes you happy," I said, hoping that his happiness would include me.

As the months passed, I realized that not only was Jay not going to make it to California, simply because he couldn't get out of his own way, but we were coming to an end as well.

It was apparent that our relationship was slowing down. We had been together for a long time, and we were seeing each other less and less. My business was going full force, and I was very busy. He quit the Medieval Manor and did some voice-overs and a few training films, but he was never able to pull the plug to get out of Boston. He almost seemed frozen in place.

Over the next year, we seemed to drift apart. It was sad, and I missed him, but I didn't want to get in the way of his success if it meant he could be happy. If he didn't want me any longer, I would deal with it. That fateful day that he said to me, "I think we should see other people," I got my answer, and I knew that was the end. From a beautiful love story to "Let's see other people," there was no going back.

12

TANQUERAY AND TONIC, TWO LIMES

"Let's go to the Hot Club!" I said to Naomi. There was a new bar in town that I had visited with some friends from work earlier that week, and I wanted to share it with her. The place was a hole-in-the-wall that seated maybe ten at the bar. "They make awesome drinks, and the place is fun."

"Okay," Naomi replied. "I'd love to check it out."

"Great. Denise is meeting us there," I said. Naomi shot me a look. "It will be fine," I said, knowing that look meant she wasn't too thrilled about seeing her. "She's coming with Chuck anyway." Chuck was Denise's boyfriend, and they were both the kind of people who always knew what—and who—was on the cutting edge. They seemed to take advantage of both to keep their social lives interesting.

Denise and Naomi could not have been more different, but they were both wonderful friends to me. Unfortunately, they didn't seem to like each other much. Denise was cute, bubbly, and outgoing, always looking for the next fun thing to do. Naomi was intellectual, and kept to herself. It wasn't easy for her to make friends. I think in some ways it was because she had a bit of a superiority complex, a sure-fire way to keep people at bay. Luckily, one of the two was always available for a night out with me, so I was happy.

We had our routine each week. Denise and I spent Monday nights at Lupo's listening to Roomful of Blues live, and any night was reserved for the Last Call Saloon, when Eight to the Bar was playing. From there it was whatever bar had a good band on those other nights. Now it looked as if the Hot Club was quickly becoming another staple in our bar scene. It was small and quiet and a needed respite in our weekly routine of crowds, dancing, and music.

Naomi and I met in the parking lot and walked into the bar together. It was cold outside and was beginning to snow. The small room adjoining the bar had a wood stove with a roaring fire, so the place was toasty.

I looked around for Denise and Chuck but didn't see them.

"Let's grab a drink," I said to Naomi, "before it gets too crazy in here." Naomi followed me to the bar.

"I'll have a Tanqueray and tonic, two limes please," I said to Josh, the bartender and establishment owner. I moved out of the way so Naomi could order.

"White wine spritzer," Naomi added.

Josh glanced up at us as he went about preparing the drinks. "These two separate?" he asked. Both Naomi and I nodded.

Naomi had a great-paying position at Rhode Island Hospital and was a whiz with money, plus she was very frugal, so always seemed to have a full wallet. As for me, I was constantly scrimping for it. It might have had something to do with my constant need to go out—after all, staying at home was no picnic, and what twentysomething girl wants to hang out with her perpetually drunk parents? It might have had to do with my working for myself and not having a steady paycheck. I started my first company at nineteen, and there was no going back. I was doing well with my catering business, but I was always the last one to be paid. After staff, expenses, and the fact that there always seemed to be something else I needed in the way of equipment, glassware, serving platters, and so on, money was tight. There were slow times as well. This was one of them.

We paid for our drinks and found a small table in the corner of the bar and sat down. It was near a pass-through to the restrooms, but at least we had a seat.

"How's business?" Naomi asked me.

"It's okay," I said, "Just quiet this time of year." It was after Christmas, and the craziness of the holiday season was over. It was the dead of winter, and things were slow. I was counting my pennies.

"It will pick up soon," Naomi said to cheer me up. "And how is Jay?" she asked.

Naomi and I were close during most of my relationship with Jay, and she knew what was going on intimately. It was obvious to her that something was not right.

I looked at her and rolled my eyes, sighing.

"Uh-oh," she said. "What's going on?" she asked.

"He's going to California," I said.

"This again?" she asked.

"Yes," I replied. "I think this is finally over," I said to her.

"I'm sorry," Naomi said to me with compassion in her eyes. She knew how much I loved him.

"I need to move on with my life. I can't keep waiting around for him," I confessed to Naomi. It was no secret that I wanted to get married and have a family and a career. Jay knew this, and we had broken up a couple of times because of it. He wanted to find his success as an actor and didn't want anything to tie him down. It didn't matter how much he loved me or how great we were together; his career was his mission. The problem was he didn't have the determination to find the success he so desired. He certainly had the talent, but the drive eluded him.

I secretly thought that he considered himself the perpetual bachelor and felt he was getting too old to give me what I wanted out of life. I was twenty-six, and he was twelve years my senior. What he obviously didn't realize was that I would have followed him anywhere. As long as we were together, I was happy. He made me feel good, content, cared for, and accepted.

"I know, but it's hard," Naomi said to me in an effort to comfort me. Naomi was not very demonstrative, but I knew she tried.

Just then, Denise walked in with Chuck, and they came over to our tiny table to say hello.

"I was just about to leave, so one of you two can have my seat if you want," I said to them. Chuck held out the seat for Denise to sit down as I got up and gathered my things.

Naomi and I headed out into the snow and went our separate ways toward home.

13

THE COLORFUL SHEEP

The phone rang, and it was Terri, my parents' neighbor. "I think your mother needs to get to the hospital!" she said.

My heart sunk. "What happened?" I asked.

"Well, I stopped over to see her this morning to replace a pack of cigarettes she let me borrow yesterday. When I answered the door—well, it's hard to explain. You just need to get home now."

"Okay, on my way," I said. This could not be good. My imagination ran wild, and Terri was not going to tell me. It could be anything. Maybe it was the cigarettes; maybe it was the nightly boozefest.

Before I left work, I called my brother, Greg, to see whether he knew anything. I was a little hesitant to reach out to him but was hoping we could still be a family and we could both work together to help our mother. He was ten years older than I and lived in the western part of New York. We lived outside of Buffalo as a family until I was nine, when we moved back to the Massachusetts–Rhode Island area. Greg was off to college in Ithaca and had been living in western New York ever since. He got away. Good for him. He and I hadn't been close since we were little kids. My mother saw to that. He was the golden boy, and I was the disappointment. I was the proverbial black sheep of the family, although I liked to think of myself more as the colorful sheep. I always thought I was on the outs mostly because I was strong willed and unconventional and sometimes had crazy ideas, but mostly I think it was because I tried to get my mother to stop drinking. She resented me for it; bourbon was her buddy.

I remember once, when I was thirteen, sitting on the hood of my father's car, crying. He came out to me and gently said, "What's the matter?"

"Why can't I get Mom to stop drinking?" I said to him.

"There is a lot to it," he said.

"But she doesn't love me. She has never said, 'I love you,' she won't hug me, and she looks at me with such hatred. What did I do? Maybe if she stops drinking so much, she will realize she loves me," I said through my tears.

"Your mother is very unhappy," he said to me with obvious pain in his eyes. He loved my mother but did not have the wherewithal to stand up to her. I knew it was tearing him apart to see me so sad. "That's why she drinks so much. To escape."

"Yes, but she has a great life, a family that loves her, a nice home. She is safe and secure. What is so bad? What did I do to deserve this?" I asked through my tears. "Why does she hate me so much?"

"She doesn't hate you, Carolyn," he said to me, wanting to hug me but just not able to bring himself to do it.

"How can any mother be so mean? She drinks so much she won't even talk to me," I said, thinking how each evening, after a few drinks, she completely ignored me. I was obviously a pest.

"I understand," my father said sadly. "Let me talk to her."

My father climbed up the few cement steps to the family room and entered the house. My mother was sitting in her favorite spot on the yellow-and-green plaid loveseat, lit cigarette in one hand, roly-poly glass with her precious bourbon in the other.

My father sat in the rocking chair near the fireplace and said, "Rose, Carolyn is upset. Can we talk about it?" I wanted so much to be close to my mother and held out hope we could still be a happy family.

My mother ignored him and continued to look forward, as if in some kind of a trance. It was most likely a bourbon trance.

"Say something, Mom!" I said to her, pleading.

"Rose, come on. Talk to us," my father said to her, pleading.

She looked over at him, then me, not saying a word.

I took that as a sign to continue. "Mom, why don't you love me? What have I done for you to hate me so much?"

Silence.

"Rose..." my father said gently but with a warning tone in his voice. "Please, this isn't fair to her."

"Mom, I don't know if I can stay here if you don't love me." It was a ridiculous threat. Where was I going to go? I was a thirteen-year-old kid with no other family that was about to take me in. Besides, everyone in our small family knew my mother had a big problem with the bottle, but it was never discussed. It was a sweep-it-under-the-rug kind of family. I was so sad and almost desperate to have some kind of assurance that my mother loved me.

She was not interested. My mother had a nervous habit of running her trembling fingers over her upper lip when she was uncomfortable. She was doing it now with gusto. Something was bothering her—most likely this line of questioning, and her guilt over not knowing why she just couldn't love her daughter.

I looked at my mother, and my heart ached. I could not understand how a mother could not love her child. But then again, I was a disappointment, not whom she had wanted as a child. She wanted another boy, and she was going to name him Alan. She told me a few times, "We had you to keep your brother company. It's too bad you were not a boy!" It was becoming apparent as I grew up I was not what she had hoped for, from statements like "You're not very smart, but that's okay—everyone can't be" to "Boys would like you more if you lost weight." Any man that would only love me for what I looked like was not someone I wanted to get to know too well.

What a way to come into the world. I just couldn't understand what I did to become so unloved. I tried to be kind, happy, and obedient. Anything to please her. Was it because I was chubby? My mother found this a great source of embarrassment. Was it because I had fair skin and freckles, and I didn't tan like she did? Apart from being called freckle-faced strawberry most of my life growing up, I liked my skin and freckles, it set me apart from everyone else. Maybe I wasn't pretty enough. It didn't matter, she didn't love me, period. I wasn't going to figure out why, even though I tried like crazy.

"Do you want me to leave? I just need to know if you love me!" I pleaded with her through stinging tears.

My mother just looked straight ahead and took another sip of her drink and completely ignored me.

"Well, there's my answer," I thought.

I gently shook my head, trying to get the memory out of my mind. I put down the phone from trying to reach my brother; there was no answer. But I left a message on his answering machine. I walked out into the main kitchen, where my coworkers were busy getting ready for an event we were running later that day.

"I've got to go," I said to Judy, one of my coworkers and sous chef.

"I've got it covered," she replied. "Take your time."

I adored the people I worked with. They were fun and talented. We worked together well and watched out for one another.

As I drove over to my mother's house, I wasn't sure what to expect. My mother saw me pull up and came over to the door as I opened it. I looked at her through the front window and strained to get a closer look. As I walked into the house, I said, "What the hell, Mom!"

Her face was covered in dried blood. There was a section of her nose hanging off, her eyes were swollen, and her clothes were covered in bloodstains. There was a gash from her temple all the way down the right side of her face, ending at her chin. There was glass embedded in her cheeks, nose and chin.

"Oh, I just had a little accident," Mom said.

"What are you talking about?" I answered, alarmed.

"I think I must have just fainted," she said sheepishly.

"Just fainted?" I asked, exasperated. "You need to go to the hospital! You need stitches."

"No, I'm fine," she said. "Why are you here?"

"Why am I here?" I said, close to a scream. "To help you! Terri called me this morning. She said that she came over to see you and you answered the door like that. She said she tried to take you to the hospital but you wouldn't go. And you're not fine, Mom. You're a mess!"

"I told her I didn't need help. I just fainted," she said.

"Get your coat. I'm taking you to the hospital right now. We're going to Miriam." Miriam Hospital was on the east side of Providence and was the hospital of choice for our family. I'm not sure why—probably because it was so close to Brown University, and our family had history at Brown.

As I walked through the dining room, I saw a huge spot of dried blood. It must have been eighteen inches in diameter. The carpet was an emerald-green color, so the dark red of the blood stood out and looked ominous.

On closer look, I saw there was one of my mother's favorite roly-poly glasses in pieces in the middle of the bloodstain. There were large shards of glass, also covered in dried blood. I picked up one of the pieces of the blood-smeared glass and brought it to my mother. "Look!" I said to her.

"Yes, I must have fallen when I fainted," she said sheepishly.

She had fallen, all right. From the position of the glass and a little detective work, I figured she must have been taking a sip as she walked back to the kitchen to refill her glass. She had tripped on the small stair leading into the dining room and fallen face first on the glass, shattering it. Then, far too drunk to get up, she had lain there and passed out.

It was a grisly sight, and the thought of it all made me sick and mad at the same time. "How could she get this bad?" I thought. "Why the slow suicide?"

I took my mother to the hospital, and the doctors looked at her. "How much were you drinking last night?" the attending physician asked her.

"Oh, just one or two drinks," she replied. My mother thought everyone was stupid enough to believe her rouse. She did this all the time. But with one look at her gray and weathered skin, it was obvious it was an understatement.

"Your liver is quite enlarged," the doctor said during the examination. "Regarding your face, you will need stitches, and maybe some plastic surgery."

My mother sneered at the words "plastic surgery." That was an extravagance, reserved for those vain "Hollywood types," as she called them. She was of strong blue-blooded stock, and she would have none of it.

The doctor dismissed me and told me they were keeping her overnight for observation. There were shards of glass in her face, possibly in her eyes, and they wanted to keep her to make sure there were no other issues. I went back home to see whether I could pick up some of the mess she had left. Once there I found Terri in the dining room, scrubbing the floor.

"Terri, you don't have to do that!" I exclaimed. "I'll take care of it later!"

"Oh, please, I don't mind. I didn't want the stain to set in," she replied.

I sat by the phone and dialed my brother again. This time he answered.

"Hi, it's Carolyn," I said to him. "Did you get my message?"

"Something about Mom going to the hospital?" he said. Terri was scrubbing away at the carpet about ten feet away. She was listening intently. This was major gossip, which she loved. I called her the Gladys Kravitz of the neighborhood.

I began to explain the situation. "Yes, you should have seen this place this morning. It looked like a crime scene. Mom passed out and fell on a glass. She's got cuts everywhere, glass embedded in her face and skin. Half her nose is falling off, and she has a gash down the side of her face. She is going to need stitches!" I stopped to take a breath. "I don't know how she lived through it. Then we found her pillow this morning also covered in blood, so she must have gotten up at some point, gone to bed, and then woken up today and ignored the whole thing."

"Well, I don't know what you want me to do about it from here," Greg replied with a haughty tone to his voice. I was flabbergasted.

"Engage in your family maybe?" I said, getting madder by the minute. "Don't leave it all for me to figure out!" There were a ton of things he could do to help. It was his mother, for heaven's sake! Then, for good measure, I added, "You're such an asshole!"

Terri immediately stopped scrubbing and perked up to listen closer. This was getting juicy. Gladys Kravitz was on alert.

"Look, Carolyn, I have my life here. There is not much I can do to help," Greg said.

"But she is a raging alcoholic! She's sick, and she needs help. She wants nothing to do with me. She will only listen to you!" I continued, getting more upset with every word. "I need some help to get her to stop drinking, or at least to start taking care of herself!" I was exasperated. My brother—the golden child my mother loved so much— was not willing to lift a finger to help her.

Greg was still living outside Buffalo with his wife, Ellie, who completely disliked everyone in our family except my brother. And sometimes I wondered about that as well. She was a bitch in every sense of the word and wore the pants in the family. I knew the words were echoing directly from her. My brother never had much of a backbone. We were kept completely away from their perfect little cocoon of a family. Ignorance was bliss to them as far as we were concerned.

"She has made her own choices in her life. There is nothing I can do to stop her from drinking. She won't stop until she's ready," he replied. Greg didn't have to endure the brunt of the drinking. It had gotten much worse after we moved back to New England, and he stayed when my father was transferred back east. My mother inherited money from a rich relative, so she didn't have to work any longer. These two things were reasons, along with loneliness and apparent self-hatred, that caused her to kick it up a notch on the alcohol scale. When my mother wasn't drunk, she was hungover. It was a vicious cycle, and she was killing herself. I think that was her point.

I was furious, sad, and exasperated. "Okay, never mind. I'll handle this on my own too," I said to him and hung up the phone. "Such a dickhead," I said under my breath. I didn't hear from him again until my mother died years later.

14

JUST ANOTHER TUESDAY NIGHT

Naomi and I were at our tiny little table at the Hot Club, having a drink. Chuck walked in with a group of guys I had never seen before. He came over to say hello as his friends went to the bar to get drinks.

"Hi, Chuck. No Denise tonight?" I asked him.

"Nope, it's men's night out tonight. I think she was doing something with her brother," he replied.

"You're here with your posse, I see. These are your friends from the ski shop?" I asked.

"Yeah, Stu and Tom," he said, pointing to two guys standing at the bar. "And Darren and Mark." He pointed to two others milling around the small crowd, sipping their cocktails, looking for a place to sit.

"Well, have fun!" I said to Chuck as he headed to the bar.

"Catch you later," he replied.

I turned back to Naomi. She and I never had a shortage of things to talk about when it came to our family. Our mothers were two of three sisters that made up the "Stanton girls." They were from a solid blue-blooded upper-middle-class family (at least they considered themselves blue bloods, a claim I had never much cared to verify), and they had married three friends from high school after World

War II. There was always some crazy drama to pick apart and analyze when it came to the Stanton girls. Naomi and I swore we would never be like them when we got older. We were determined to live more normal, unpretentious lives. So far, so good, but we had a long way to go to prove we could do it.

"Sorry," I said to Naomi. "Now, where were we?"

"We were talking about your mother," she replied.

"Oh, right. What can I do about this? Am I allowed legally to get her into rehab, make her dry out somehow?" I continued. I was desperate to find a way to help my mother stop drinking. It was killing her. It seemed to me like a ridiculous cycle of despair, which unfortunately she didn't seem to mind one bit. I found out later that my mother had been in love with a man who died in World War II, and she married my father because he was the next best thing. I felt so bad for my dad—he didn't deserve to be so unhappy—and together it was a miserable match.

"She will never stop drinking if it is not her idea. Unless she wants to stop," Naomi said. "You can't make her do anything she doesn't want to, legally or otherwise." Naomi knew how stubborn my mother was. I was looking for her opinion as a health care provider who maybe knew something I didn't about this. I didn't like the answer.

"And therein lies the problem," I replied to Naomi sadly. "She doesn't want to stop. Bourbon is her best friend." My mother's drinking was such a source of shame for me. I tried to hide it from almost everyone, and did pretty well up to a point. But Naomi was my cousin and knew firsthand what my mother was all about.

"I can't even tell you how much she drank last week, but it was an insane amount. She buys a half gallon plus one bottle on Fridays, then is back Tuesday afternoon for more. It's sickening," I explained to Naomi. "I don't know how she is still alive." I was getting more depressed by the minute.

"It must be that superior blue blood of theirs," Naomi said, laughing. I rolled my eyes at her.

"I have got to get out of that house. I just can't afford it yet. I guess I should be grateful, and I am, that I have a place to live while I try to build my business. Maybe I should just get a real job," I stated.

"Carolyn, you know you would be miserable in a nine-to-five job or in a cubicle somewhere," Naomi warned. "You are an entrepreneur and need to do things your way. Besides, you're really good at what you do." She was trying to tell me in a nice way that I was too stubborn to work for anyone else. She also knew I could no more do a job like hers than she could do a job like mine. She knew I worked harder than most people but had a lot less to show for it in the way of monetary resources.

"I just would hate to leave my father alone. He's so sad all the time," I continued. "Okay, enough of that. Let's get positive. What's going on with you?"

"Okay, but we can talk about it more later if you want," Naomi said, looking at me with sympathy. "Let's see. I'm filling in as head nurse on our floor while my boss is on vacation."

"Awesome!" I said happily, glad there was some good news. "You should be proud of yourself!"

"Well, it's just while she is on vacation. But it's a step in the right direction," she said.

"Sure is, and once they find out how smart you are, they won't want you to leave the position." I was happy for Naomi but also a little jealous. She had her life together, or at least seemed to. Everything in its place. No worries. My life, on the other hand, seemed like a complete disaster.

"We'll see," Naomi said, snuffing out her cigarette. She looked up at me as I got up to see how long the line to the ladies' room was. I saw her glance behind me. I turned around and saw Chuck approaching the table with one of the guys from the ski shop.

"Hey, Carolyn and Naomi. This is Tom." Chuck introduced us to an average-looking guy who seemed pretty quiet but had the most beautiful-colored brown eyes.

"Hi," Tom said back, pausing for a moment but barely looking at us as he continued to the men's room around the corner. He didn't seem to be able to look us straight in the eye. To me that meant that he either was very shy or had something to hide.

Chuck continued. "We were just on the way out to hit another bar, and I wanted to stop by and say good-bye, and Tom had to hit the head." I thought the word "head" was such a ridiculous name. I wondered how the nautical name for bathroom was conceived. I'd have to look that up when I had a minute.

"Where to next?" I asked.

"Just across the street to the Wine Bar. We may be back," Chuck answered.

"Okay, maybe we'll see you later then." My life at this point was a never-ending cycle of bars, cocktails, friends, friends of friends, who was where, who was going where, and how they were going to get to where they were headed. It was certainly fun but seemed to have no stability whatsoever.

I was anxious for them to leave; I wanted to get back to my conversation with Naomi.

They left, and Chuck waved as he walked out the door of the tiny space. I turned back to Naomi as we continued our conversation.

"So do you miss Jay?" Naomi asked me after they left.

"I have to admit I do. We were so good together," I replied with a sigh. "I don't know, Naomi. I loved him so much, but we want different things. I don't want to stand in his way. He wants to continue with his career. I'm working all the time. My little business is doing okay. I can't just leave and go with him to the West Coast. Besides, he never asked me."

"I know it's tough. Oh, I forgot to tell you—I saw his friend Kenny a couple of weeks ago, and we were talking about Jay," Naomi started.

That hurt a little bit, to hear about him from someone else. I used to know everything that was going on in his life. "Oh?" I said.

"Yes, and Kenny told me that he was dating a girl who looked kind of like you—blue eyes and strawberry-blond hair—and you will never believe this…"

"What?" I asked, not really wanting the answer.

Naomi looked at me and said, "Her name is Carolyn."

15

IT WAS ALL PLANNED

"That was planned, you know," Chuck said as I answered the phone.

"What was planned?" I asked.

"Tom and that little side trip to the men's room last night," he replied. "He thinks you're cute. He wanted to meet you."

"Really? Well, you would never know it," I argued. "He barely looked at us and maybe said one word to me."

"He's a good guy, Carolyn. Maybe a little shy, but a good guy," Chuck said.

"I thought the other guy you came in with, Mark—was that his name? He was cute," I responded.

"Yes, and so does every other girl in Rhode Island. Stay away from him. He's a lady-killer and an asshole to women," Chuck replied. I could tell Chuck was acting as big brother to me. I appreciated it; he was a good friend. "Tom wants to know if you will be at the Hot Club Friday night. When we get out of work, around nine thirty."

"Probably," I said.

"Great. We'll see you there," Chuck responded.

"Okay, but Chuck?" I asked.

"Yes?" he replied.

"Already, I'm not impressed," I said and hung up the phone. I would give it a try and see where it went. I had to at least give this guy Tom the benefit of the doubt.

Friday night came, and Naomi, Denise, and I were crammed at our little table in the corner. Most nights it was on our partying agenda, we got there early to find a seat. I was at the bar ordering a drink. Chuck came up behind me and put his hands over my eyes from behind.

"Guess who," he said.

"I can't imagine," I replied sarcastically but with a big smile.

He released his hands from my eyes, and I turned around to find both Chuck and Tom behind me. We all smiled and said hello to one another.

"I've got to find the other guys," Chuck said and wandered off.

"How convenient," I thought.

Tom stayed behind and asked me what I was drinking. "Tanqueray and tonic with two limes," I replied. He ordered himself a drink as well, and we talked at the bar for a little while. As the crowd thinned out, we moved into the little room by the docks outside and sat by the wood stove. It was just the two of us out there. I seemed to be doing most of the talking. I talked about my business, what I was hoping to accomplish, my background a little, and where I'd lived. I avoided all talk of my family.

I learned about Tom too. He was from Barrington and had lived there most of his life, went to Bentley College, got a degree in management and accounting, and worked for a large corporation. I knew my mother would love him. He was everything I was supposed to have in a mate. He had all the signs that he could provide me with a good, predictable life. Or so I had been told by my mother since I was a little girl. Find the right boy. Which meant from the right family, the right town, whatever was "right" in her pickled brain. Love had nothing to do with it. It was more about my living a life my mother could brag to her friends and sisters about.

"This might work," I thought to myself. He seemed nice and steady, and he seemed to genuinely like me. I was getting tired of my tumultuous life. Maybe it was time for something new. Calmer. Steadier. "Let's see where this goes," I thought to myself.

Chuck called me the next day around noon.

"He thinks you're awesome!" Chuck said. "Actually, those were his exact words. I've never seen him so excited about anything."

"That's good," I replied. "He seemed nice."

Chuck replied, "Well, I hope you think he is more than nice. He's crazy about you, just after one night talking."

"I could, Chuck. I think I definitely could," I replied.

That following week, Tom and I went on our first date. He took me to the Chart House in Newport. It was a nice evening. He was a perfect gentleman, well dressed and attentive. He opened the car door for me and was gracious at dinner, even sharing with me the most succulent piece of his lobster. It was everything a perfect date should be.

Unfortunately, most of the evening there was no zip, no excitement, no fun. Our conversations were dry and unspirited. I chalked it up to his shyness and figured it would get better as we got to know each other. We talked a bit about his family, who were incredibly close and happy, did lots of fun things together, and actually seemed to like one another. They seemed happy and just about perfect in every way—a family just like I had wished for, for as long as I could remember.

Tom and I dated a couple of times a week for months. Our uneventful conversations didn't get much more interesting. I think I was entertainment for him sometimes. It was starting to become obvious that he was falling in love with me. I was starting to love him as well, as I slowly got to know him.

We had a great time as a group with his friends, who were a rowdy, fun group of skiers, sailors, and surfers. The kind of people I felt I would never belong with—the beautiful people. Tom was wonderful to me, and I felt safe, cared for. I had a nice man—with a good job, who wore all the right clothes and knew all the right people—paying attention to me. And he stayed around, despite the fact that he had met my parents. He didn't seem to mind them. My shame was so deep that the simple fact that Tom accepted them for who they were earned huge points in his favor.

As time went on and we continued to stay together, I buried the fact that there was no real, deep soul-level connection between us. It all looked great on the surface, and I loved being included in his world. The fact that a deep connection with love and passion was nowhere to be found in our relationship made me sad and empty. I knew I wasn't going to have that type of relationship again and knew I had to deal with it and appreciate what I did have. And besides, I believed Tom loved me as much as he could love anyone.

One night, after going to the movies to see *The Breakfast Club*—which was an almost-impossible feat to convince Tommie to do—we headed up to Providence to stop by the Hot Club for a nightcap. I was calling him Tommie by this time; it seemed to fit him, and it stuck. We had one drink, he a bourbon on the rocks (which I couldn't stand the smell of, for obvious reasons), and I a stinger on the rocks. We sat there and took in the surroundings. It was a thin crowd and quiet for a change. It was Tuesday night.

We finished our drinks and walked out to the car. I leaned up against the car as his hand reached for the passenger-side door to open it for me. He leaned in to kiss me as I kissed him back. The kiss was okay; it was nothing special, almost obligatory, and I seemed to be doing most of the work. I opened my eyes slightly; something didn't seem right. What I found was a man who was wide eyed, looking at something across the parking lot. He was checking something out. "What the hell?" I thought.

I pulled away and looked at him. He was a bit startled at my abruptness and said in a snarky tone, "What?"

"What the hell are you looking at?" I asked him, annoyed.

He had the look of a kid getting caught with his hand in the cookie jar and said sheepishly, "I was looking at the compressor on that building across the parking lot." I followed his line of sight and saw a huge square metal contraption. Now I had no idea what a compressor was, and I wasn't interested in finding out. All I knew was that during our kiss, here was this man checking out a piece of equipment that he found more appealing than me. A stupid hunk of metal!

"What is so interesting about that?" I asked, still very annoyed.

"Nothing. Sorry. Come here," he said, chuckling as he tried to pull me closer to kiss him and pick up where we left off. He thought it was funny, which it might have been with other people or in other circumstances, but there wasn't a whole lot of passion to our relationship, so this was another wake-up call to how little depth our relationship really had.

"How very romantic. I'm sorry I am not as interesting as whatever that thing is," I said.

"Carolyn, come on. I'm sorry," he said, not really understanding why he was apologizing. "But what's the big deal?"

I looked at him, and the word "clueless" popped into my head as I walked back into the bar. "I will find my own ride home."

What happened next was a preview of what our entire relationship would be like. He left. He didn't go back into the bar to find me to talk it through or apologize. He just walked away. He thought he was right, so he was dismissing the situation by chalking it up to an overreaction on my part. He also justified leaving because he had to get up early for work the next day. Work was everything. It came above all else.

Later that week I met up with Abby, Tom's sister. "I've been thinking about breaking up with Tommie," I said to her. Abby and I had become friends while Tom and I were dating. She and I were about the same age and had struck up a mild friendship. This evening, it was just she and I at the bar; it was early, and the sun was just going down. No one else had arrived at our favorite drinking spot yet.

Abby looked at me. "You know this means we won't be friends anymore," she said.

"What are you talking about?" I asked.

"It's just the way it is. If you stop dating Tom, we can't hang out," she replied. I didn't agree with her that that was just the way things were, but obviously to her, that would be that.

Abby didn't mean it as a threat; she was too matter of fact for that. She had her opinions, and those were the only ones that mattered to her—and as far as she was concerned, the only ones there were, period.

The thought put a little panic in me. I had found a nice family to be a part of, a family to connect to and feel loved by. This was something that had eluded me most of my life, and I didn't want to lose it. Tom's mother was wonderful and had a quiet wisdom I began to cherish. His father was strong, funny, and in command at all times. He was an interesting man who tried lots of new things. He loved the fact that I was a chef, and we often talked about cooking. He asked me for advice on some recipes and methodology. It was nice to commiserate and be respected for something I was good at. I didn't want to lose this happy little family I was becoming so attached to, but Tom and I just didn't connect on a deep level. Even our conversations had no depth; they were about the tasks of the day and current events.

"I guess..." I said to Abby.

"Why do you want to break up with him?" she asked.

"I don't know. It just seems like he doesn't care about me that much. He just likes having me around for entertainment or a prize or something." At that point in my life, I was in my late twenties. I was fun, attractive, and thin—at least as thin as I was ever going to be. I attracted lots of attention from men, mostly because I was easy to talk to and had an outgoing personality.

To me, my problem was that I needed to find someone that would take me as I was, crazy family and all; therefore, I couldn't be too picky.

"What are you talking about? He's always around you, takes you everywhere!" Abby retorted. "And if you don't have plans, he's in here every night looking for you."

"I know. He walks through the bar, scoping out the place with his ski buddies, sees me, sits down, says hello, and doesn't say another word. Just sits there. I do all the talking. It's boring." I felt bad saying this to his sister, but it was true. "Do you know what he did last night?" I asked.

"No, what? Tell me," Abby said.

"We were outside," I began, "and he leaned over to kiss me goodnight. It was an okay kiss, but there was absolutely no feeling behind it. It seemed mechanical almost, and cold."

"And?" Abby said, getting annoyed.

"And as if that wasn't enough to make me wonder, I opened my eyes during the kiss and saw him, with his eyes wide open, looking at the compressor on the building next door!" I said, frustrated, pointing to the huge metal contraption out the window. "He was actually checking this thing out!" I said, wide eyed, trying hard to get my point across. "I obviously was not as interesting as that thing!"

"Well, at least it wasn't another girl," Abby said, kidding with me. She didn't get it either. Must have been a family thing.

"That doesn't help, Abby," I said and looked down at my drink, taking a sip.

16

I GUESS I COULD

Tom and I ended up staying together. It was comfortable. We got into a routine that was fun, if predictable, and went about our lives each day.

Tom knew how horrible things were at my house. He didn't want to talk about it and got a bit annoyed with me if I prattled on about it too much, but he put up with it for the most part.

"I was thinking maybe you would like to move in here with me." Tom was comfortable having me around, and I knew he loved me.

"Hmm..." I said. "That might be nice."

"You will have to pay rent though," he said. "Maybe around eight hundred dollars a month." Looking back on that now, that would have covered his mortgage. He was always thinking like a businessman.

Tommie had just purchased a small condo on the water in Wickford. It was adorable and needed some updating, but it was a perfect first home for him. He had stayed with his parents until he was about thirty, saving his money while working two jobs. It worked for him, and he was excited to move into his new place.

"Okay, I'll do my best," I said but knew I would never be able to afford to do it, but I would try. I was just glad he had asked me. I was excited to create a little home for us. Somehow, I would make it work. I was never good with money, and it usually burned a hole in my pocket. (I could hear my mother saying that to me time and time again, along with her standard "It's okay you're not very smart—everyone can't be.") Years later when I began to go through my spiritual awakening, I realized that I believed anything she said to me was accurate, and I was who she thought me to be, whether it was true or not. Good, bad, or indifferent, she shaped my self-image. The effect a parent can have on a child is a powerful thing. I finally learned that I had to be very careful of my thoughts, as it repeatedly manifested into my reality.

We lived in the little condo for months; we often had parties and had friends over, mostly his friends. I never did pay any rent specifically, but did contribute to the household in many other ways. I continued cooking and growing my business, and Tom worked for a large corporation, so we had some stability. We started to really bond with each other. I was falling in love with him. It was not the same kind of love I had with Jay, which was free, easy, and deep, but it was love just the same. Our kind of love. It was a wonderful time.

Sex with Tom was good, and certainly satisfying, but it was almost clinical. It felt as if he was thinking about something he had read in *Playboy* and decided he would try out. It wasn't very emotional, and he seemed to be thinking about what he was doing most of the time. At least he had the mechanics of it figured out.

One night, we were relaxed and lying in bed after making love. "What would you say if I asked you to marry me?" Tom asked before we both fell asleep. I knew the question was coming, but I secretly wished there would be some romance, or at least some thought put into it.

Now the first response to pop into my head was "Why don't you ask and find out?" but this was no time for a snarky remark. This was serious, and I knew Tom would not think it was funny.

"I would probably say yes," I responded.

"Okay, good," he replied. "So when should we do it?"

So that was that. We were engaged.

17

AFTER THE DRIFT

Jay called me from time to time over the years after we drifted apart. I wanted him to be happy, to find his way as an actor. He wanted me to be happy, finding my life with a home, children, and the white picket fence. He often asked me to come up to see him, and sometimes I did. We met at the Medieval Manor, where he was working again, on and off, a couple of times to have a drink after a performance. Sometimes we would meet for lunch in Boston at Faneuil Hall or go see a movie. He always let me know when he had a live performance somewhere. He called me every Christmas and on my birthday to let me know he was thinking about me, and whenever *It's a Wonderful Life* came on TV. It was his favorite movie, and he wanted to make sure I watched it.

It was confusing. But I loved being with him; we had deep, wonderful conversations and laughed all the time. He was so funny and great to be around. I missed being part of his daily life.

Whenever I was with him, I felt at peace. Happy. It had been years since we were together, and he still had not left for California. He had broken up with Cally—the other Carolyn. He was mad at her for leaving him for another man. Jay did admit to me that she realized his heart was somewhere else. On the surface, he was pretending to be happy, but I knew he wasn't content with his life.

One day, when Tom was gone on one of his regular trips, I decided to drive up to Boston to see Jay. I wanted to talk with him in person and tell him that I was engaged. "I'm getting married," I said to him nervously as we sat in my car outside his apartment building. He was leaving for a performance in about twenty minutes, so it was a rushed but necessary conversation.

"Are you sure he is the right man for you?" he asked. "Do you love him?"

"No, I love you, but you don't seem to want me, and you will probably never get your act together anyway!" I thought. What came out of my mouth was "Of course I love him."

"So you found a suitable husband from Beaver Cleaver Land?" Jay sniped. He often used Cleaver-family analogies, from the *Leave It to Beaver* TV show from the early sixties. "I bet you only have sex in the missionary position."

"Oh, for heaven's sake, Jay, is that all you think about?" I said to him, annoyed. "It's not true. Plus it's none of your business," I said back, aggravated. "I just wanted to let you know I was getting married so you would hear it from me and not through the grapevine." My grapevine and Jay's grapevine didn't intersect much anymore, but we did still have some mutual friends, and I owed it to him to tell him in person.

Secretly I hoped that this would make him realize that he was going to lose me for good. Maybe jar him into realizing that we could find a way to make this work.

I did love Tom. He was good to me; it was just a different kind of love. He wanted to marry me and make me part of his life. Would I have the deep connection and passion I had with Jay? No. But Jay wasn't interested in marriage; that was obvious. I was, and I wanted a happy family with kids, Sunday dinner, all of it. I just wanted to feel part of something, connected to someone to love so we could take care of each other. It's interesting to think about the choices we make and how they influence the rest of our lives. At that point in my life, I felt as if choices were becoming less and less available to me.

Jay looked at me, searching my face and for the words to reply. Not finding the right words was not a problem he had very often. He always knew what to say and how to say it to get his point across. Now he was silent; what I said to him seemed to be sinking in.

"Jay, you don't love me anymore, and we want different things," I continued, mad at myself for sounding like a forlorn schoolgirl.

"Yes, I do love you, Carolyn. I'm just not in love with you," Jay finally said. There it was, his admission. It hurt to hear the words. It sounded as if he had been rehearsing those words for just such an occasion.

"That's just not enough," I replied, thinking that Jay couldn't seem to make up his mind about me or the career in California he was stalling to create. He seemed to be frozen—wanting both at the same time and doing neither.

Jay hesitated. "Well, just make sure he's good to you. And let him know that if he does anything to hurt you, he'll have me to answer to," he said seriously. "Call me anytime, for anything."

That sounded funny coming from him. Jay was passive, peaceful. Aggression was not his style. I could tell he was not at all pleased with my news, but he also didn't want to stand in my way. I think he suspected that it did make me happy, on some level.

"Take care of yourself," I replied. "And good luck on the West Coast. I wish you joy and success and really hope you find what you are looking for." He had so many opportunities, so much talent. I still hoped and dreamed about his making it, finding his bliss—whatever that looked like—and then he would come back to me. Unfortunately, it seemed like a pipe dream.

"I will. Thanks," Jay said. That was that. No fighting for me, no pleading me to stay with him. It was sad, and it was over.

18

TWINKLE TOES

The wedding was a dream come true for me. The event itself, anyway. It was held at a very old church, which had seen the baptisms of many generations of our family. The setting was spectacular, with eight bridesmaids and eight ushers in attendance.

Standing at the back of the church, before walking down the aisle, I was tightly holding my father up to support him. He didn't feel well, as he had been diagnosed with a blood disorder, and he was also a nervous wreck. As I looked down the aisle of the church, I wondered to myself how long this marriage would last. I was happy but didn't feel any real joy, and I was resigned to the fact that this was my future. Also, I had to pee. What else was new? I always had to pee when I was nervous. And I was very nervous about this marriage.

My company was catering the reception—a seven-course meal that my staff were working hard to create. I loved these guys; they all pulled together to make an incredible day. The food, at least, was spectacular.

I catered it mostly to save my parents money. They didn't have the financial resources to pay for much more than tea and scones. But I wanted a beautiful wedding and a wonderful celebration of our day for my friends and extended family. So it was up to me to make it happen. My father had lost his job when the printing plant he managed closed, and my mother had stopped working. I think it was interfering with her drinking. But the money she had inherited was held up in a trust, so she didn't have a lot of disposable income. What she did have went to bills and booze.

To make it all come together, along with my staff, I enrolled the help of many of my culinary friends, chefs, and pastry chefs. Our menu was carefully designed to offer some of our best dishes and show off our talents. We were going for the *wow* factor.

After cocktails and hors d'oeuvres were served on the main floor of the casino at Roger Williams Park, the guests were escorted upstairs to the formal dining room, where dinner would be served. The courses consisted of a creamy lobster chowder and oysters Rockefeller, followed by tortellini carbonara with prosciutto and pecorino Romano cheese. Then came Caesar salad with shaved Parmesan crisps and ciabatta croutons, followed by a palate cleanser of lemon sorbet. The main course was charcoal-grilled filet mignon au poivre with red-bliss potatoes roasted in garlic and shallots, and grilled asparagus drizzled lightly with olive oil and sea salt. For dessert, we served white-chocolate mousse with fresh raspberries tossed in Chambord.

While dessert and coffee were being served, each table was served a silver tray with a tall martini glass containing softly whipped cream and small nips of cordials so the guests could make their own international coffees. Our friends especially loved this, and many pockets were clinking and full of the nips that weren't consumed, most likely to be added to their travel mugs for the ski trip many of our friends were going on early the next morning.

Our wedding cake was a toasted hazelnut cake with vanilla-hazelnut buttercream layered with milk chocolate ganache. We all ate well that day.

During the reception, the band made a big deal about our first dance, and Tommie and I went up to the dance floor. I loved to dance, loved all music; it spoke to me on a very deep level. It always seemed to put me in a state of complete joy. Tom, on the other hand, didn't have a musical bone in his body. But it was expected of us, so we were going to give it a go.

We had hired a swing band to play at our reception; they were wonderful, and the music was fun. My father loved swing music, and that was one of the main reasons I hired them. I loved to make my father happy. He was my rock, one of the only positive things in my home life. One of his favorite sayings was "No problem!" and he really believed there were no problems that couldn't be figured out. His other favorite saying was "Everything is negotiable," and I guess those two thoughts went hand in hand. He was also very much behind the women's movement for years before it was a cool thing to do. He often told me he believed women were the superior gender. "Men have nothing over women," he would say, and he really believed it.

As Tom and I stood there, all eyes were on us as the band played "Someone to Watch over Me," and we started to dance. Tom was counting the steps, concentrating hard, and I was just feeling the music, happy to be in the moment. I looked lovingly into his eyes; he was concentrating on his feet.

"What are you doing?" he said to me as we stumbled, out of sync with the beat and each other. "You're not doing it right!"

"Not doing what right?" I said, laughing. "I just want to dance!" I thought he was kidding. He was not.

"Well, you're messing up. I took ballroom dance lessons when I was a kid," he said as he tried to right his steps. "I know how to do this!"

I looked at him and saw that he was actually mad at me. Frustrated. There we were, on the dance floor at our wedding, and he was upset with me for not dancing the way he thought I should. A lump swelled up in my throat, and I just walked away, hurt, realizing there was not going to be any romance that day. Or any other, as I came to find out. I was wondering what I had gotten myself into, and this wasn't a good start.

The dance floor was filling up, and everyone was having a great time, so I slipped away to head to the first floor, where the commercial kitchens were located. I went down to see my staff and friends that were working so hard to make the day wonderful.

"What are you doing in here?" Glenn asked me. He was running the show, and he couldn't believe I was in the middle of the kitchen, practically behind the serving line, in my wedding dress.

"Oh, it's only a dress. Besides, I just had to come down and see you all and thank you!" I said, hugging him and anyone else I could find. "You all did such an incredible job on everything. It was all so perfect!" I gushed. These guys had pulled off something incredible, and I was touched and loved them even more for it.

"Glad you are so happy!" Glenn said, smiling and quickly hugging me back, wanting to get back to work. "Everything is going great here, so get back upstairs to your guests."

"Okay, okay, and thank you so much, everyone! There is some champagne in the walk-in fridge for you guys! Enjoy!"

Everyone waved and offered congratulations. I headed back upstairs to the guests.

Just before we left for the evening, Tom and I walked up to his sisters to say good-bye. Both were in the wedding, but Abby was mad at me because I didn't pair her up with the person she wanted me to. As we walked over, I smiled at them with genuine happiness overflowing from my heart. I was so glad that we were going to be a big happy family. I said to Tom's sisters, Abby and Jean, "We're sisters now," as I hugged them. Jean smiled and hugged me back. Abby simply wanted to correct me and said, "No, we're sisters-in-law." That was how it was going to be from then on. The lines were drawn.

19

THERE WILL BE NO HUG

The following years were lonely.

Tom was laid off from his corporate job, and as he looked for work, he applied only for positions that included travel. He didn't want to work near home; he wanted to be on the road, no matter what that meant. In the past, he did everything from furniture sales to consulting to becoming a ship's captain and delivering small cruise ships around the United States. Anything to be away from home, and me. I would often ask him why he wouldn't look for work so he could stay at home.

"There is no local work for someone with my experience," he would say. I never understood it; with a degree in management and accounting from a great school, he could surely find something. And we lived less than an hour from Boston. It just never made sense.

As I raised our children, Tom didn't partake in much. He had his life—I had mine. That's the way he wanted it. I was working full time, taking care of the kids, and he came home late Friday nights and left Sunday afternoons. Week in, week out. He refused to look for work that would allow him to stay home. He wanted his freedom, and his family part time.

Most of our marriage was conditional. If I was doing well and successful in business or was making good money, he was content. If I was struggling, he withheld his affection.

One beautiful autumn day, the air was filled with the smell of leaves and pumpkins. I was making dinner for the family, there was a fire crackling in the fireplace, and I was beaming with happiness. I just loved days like this. My sister-in-law and I were talking about what we were going to do for a menu for Thanksgiving, besides the obligatory turkey and stuffing. We typically had the holiday at our house, and I loved to have everyone together as a family. I lived for that feeling. I could deal with my unhappy marriage as long as I had a happy family around me for the holidays.

"I can do the carrots and turnips and make a dessert," Jean said. "Why don't you ask Tommie to make something this year? You have so much to do with everything else and getting the family together here." We usually had twenty-two to twenty-four people, and it was cramped, but we had a good time.

"Tom refuses to cook," I said to Jean. "I've tried to get him to pitch in, to make dinner, breakfast, anything. He'll cook for himself if he absolutely has to, and then it's only Saugy hotdogs or a grilled cheese. Otherwise, it is up to me."

"He used to make brownies when he was a kid," Jean said. "He must figure he is no match for you."

"Maybe," I said, thinking she was probably right. Maybe he was jealous. I could cook up a storm for our friends and family, and everyone would compliment me left and right. He loved the fact that his wife was being complimented, but he would never say anything himself. This man was hard to please when it came to me. Withholding love and affection was his weapon against me. For what reason he felt he needed weapons, I had no idea.

It was the holiday season, and I was feeling great. I saw Tommie outside raking the leaves and went out to see him. I came up behind him and wrapped my arms around him from behind to give him a hug. I had love and happiness bursting from me and wanted to show my affection.

"Huh? What the hell!" he said to me, turning around quickly, recoiling from my hug as I stumbled backwards.

"I just wanted to give you a hug!" I said, smarting from the reaction, and I put my arms down and backed away slightly.

"You startled me—I am trying to get some work done!" Tommie said to me furiously. A lump rose in my throat, and I just couldn't understand how I could be so annoying to him. I didn't know what I had done. I just knew I would try to make it better. I would work harder. Be nicer. Surely, he must love me; he married me, after all.

20

BED AND BEACH

Jay called me at work, and we talked for a while. I had called him the evening before, after many months when I was lonely and sad. I just wanted to hear his voice, talk with someone who was present in a conversation, someone who understood me, cared about me.

He was still not married and didn't seem to have anyone special in his life. He was doing well with commercials and voice-overs but was still in Boston, in the same third-floor walk-up he had been in for years.

We exchanged pleasantries with an ease only Jay could accomplish with me. "How are you really?" he asked me after a few minutes of getting caught up.

"I'm okay," I replied.

"Carolyn," he said in a cautionary tone. "It's me you're talking to. What is going on?"

I explained to him how sad I was, and lonely, and that I just wanted to talk with him, to connect again. I missed him. No strings attached.

"I would love to see you," he said to me. "Do you want me to drive down? We can talk..."

"Cheating!" I thought to myself. I couldn't do it. It was not my style, and I could not bring myself to hurt Tom, no matter how empty our marriage was. Then again, I was kidding myself. What I was doing was already cheating. I didn't have to be sleeping with Jay to be cheating. My heart was not with my husband; it was still with Jay, despite our circumstances.

"But I have Tristan," I said. I was certainly not going to include my two-year-old son in this behavior.

"Well, if we are ever together, your son should get to know me," Jay replied.

I wondered where that statement had come from. Obviously, Jay had thought about this. Did he still actually think we would be together? The thought of it made me hopeful, but it did seem ridiculous.

Jay and I saw each other off and on after that. Tom was always away, so it filled in some lonely hours, and I loved to be around him. He was fun and easy to be with and had such wonderful friends that adored him. I think they all knew what was going on, but they just wanted Jay to be happy. And if I was going to do that for him, that's all they cared about. They welcomed me back into their group gracefully. Unfortunately, the guilt I was feeling overshadowed any happiness I had from our visits together. But that didn't stop me; I was desperate to feel something.

We played poker, had dinner together, went to the Boston aquarium, and walked around Faneuil Hall, watching the street performers and window shopping. He was a perfect gentleman, except for a few meaningful kisses here and there, but I set him straight. It was all just friends hanging out together—or so I told myself. No sex involved, so I was still being faithful. He respected the fact that I was married. Until he changed his mind.

"Meet me at my apartment at eight a.m.," Jay said to me when he called to check to see whether we were still going to see each other that coming weekend to do something. Tristan was staying with his grandmother, and Tom was on one of his never-ending trips for work. I found myself free of restraints.

The ocean was my blissful place. I loved the sights, sounds, and smells of it. Jay knew this and surprised me with a day-trip to my favorite spot in Maine.

It was November and cold but sunny. We walked along Ogunquit Beach huddled next to each other from the cold, listening to the waves, smelling the sea air, and watching the sea gulls circling above, when Jay announced to me, "I have a surprise for you."

"You do?" I answered. I love surprises.

"Mmm, I do," he said in his incredibly sexy and melodic voice. "I have a room at the hotel here on the beach for us."

"But Jay..." I said. My heart was in my throat. I was instantly nervous.

"How could I not? You have a whole weekend to yourself, and I want to hold you, please you. I miss you."

"We've seen each other a lot!" I said to him, knowing my argument had little substance. "I love our time together just as it is," I continued, although it was evident I had to muster the conviction to make it sound convincing.

I didn't know what was more prevalent in my mind at that minute: how much I wanted Jay or that I would be cheating on my husband. The loneliness of my empty marriage overtook me, and I just smiled at him. Jay studied my face with his "I'm going to devour you" look, turned me around on the quiet and empty beach, and led me back toward the hotel.

After about two minutes, as we lay on the bed kissing, I became very antsy. "Jay, this isn't right," I said, pushing him away. He stopped kissing me for a moment and looked at me with dreamy eyes. His mind was far away. He did not want to be interrupted.

"Come on. It's okay, honey. Come back here, and lie down next to me," he said as he pulled me closer.

"'Honey'?" I thought. "You don't have the right to call me that anymore." It didn't feel good, and I felt completely guilty. It was not helping my loneliness; it just felt shameful.

"I can't," I said. "I didn't know you had this planned, and anyway, it just isn't right!"

"We have a hotel room, a weekend alone, and nowhere to be." It was apparent that Jay had been hoping for just this opportunity. "We're so good together."

I gave in with a sigh, and we began kissing again. Within a few seconds, I bolted off the bed and said loudly, "No! I just can't do this, Jay!"

Jay realized I was determined, more determined than he was at that point. "Okay, but it seems like such a waste of a good hotel room." He was trying to be funny, but I was too upset, nervous, and consumed with guilt.

"I have to go," I said, grabbed my coat, and headed out of the hotel room toward a pay phone I saw at the end of the row of rooms. I called Tom and told him I loved him and asked, "When are you coming home?" I was so confused. I looked to the heavens and asked aloud, "What is going on!" Even then I knew there was a bigger plan to my little life here on earth, and at that point, none of it made sense.

After that episode at Ogunquit Beach, I didn't see Jay for a long time. I couldn't do it anymore, not even casually. It wasn't fair to Tom or our son, or Jay, for that matter. I would just have to deal with the unhappiness and try hard to make it all work.

As much as I loved seeing Jay and spending time with him, he was never going to be just a friend. After the love and deep passion that we shared, he would always be so much more than that to me. And that was just too dangerous. I wanted him all or nothing. It looked as if it was going to have to be nothing.

Tom and I went about our predictable lives. I enjoyed life as much as I could but fell into a deep depression. I didn't feel much of anything, just emptiness most of the time. I never smiled, and I had a constant feeling of dread. After a while, I could not even get out of bed in the morning and didn't know what to do about it. It felt hopeless. I couldn't shake the feeling and didn't know how to change it. I knew it wasn't fair to Tristan, but Tom didn't seem to notice, or at the least didn't want to address the problem. I began taking an antidepressant my doctor prescribed for me, and it helped quite a bit to raise my mood but did nothing for the feeling of a heavy heart.

Things slowly got better from there. The best part of my life was my wonderful son, Tristan. He and I grew so close; we were best friends and did everything together. We laughed and hugged and snuggled every night. I loved this little person so much, and it was beautiful to see him grow into his personality, and see glimpses of the kind of person he was going to become.

21

FLIPPED

It was January, and it was my thirty-third birthday. I called it my Rolling Rock birthday because of the number thirty-three on the inside of the label and because it was my favorite beer at the time.

I was planning on going out with a couple of friends, Jack and Denise, and we were going to check out the new Brew Pub in Providence.

Jay called me to wish me a happy birthday, as he did every year. "Are you doing anything special tonight?" he asked.

"I was going to go to the new Brew Pub in Providence with some friends," I replied.

"Oh, that sounds like fun," he said.

"Do you want to join us?" I asked before I could think about the consequences of the invitation. "What are you doing, Carolyn?" I thought to myself as soon as it came out of my mouth.

"I may just do that," he said.

"Great," I said, trying not to sound too excited. "It's near Union Station and the Capital Grille. Maybe I'll see you later."

We hung up the phone, and I thought about what to do. Tom was working but would be flying home and wanted to join us later, which was the last thing I wanted him to do. We were so unhappy in our marriage, and he put such a damper on any evening out. He didn't like my friends, always had snide comments about them, and could be downright unkind. I didn't want him to ruin my birthday. I felt terrible about it, but I wanted to have fun without worrying about what he thought all evening. It was my birthday, damn it! I wanted to do what I wanted to do.

Most of my friends didn't understand what I saw in Tom or why we were together. Our communication seemed to revolve around who could antagonize the other more. I had left him once and asked him for a divorce a couple of times, but he would just say, "Let's wait and see." I thought he didn't want to divorce me because it would cost him too much, and since he was traveling all the time and I was home taking care of things, it worked out for him—so why stop? I could have left him, walked out, but by that time I had no support system whatsoever, no family, no steady work. I closed my company after fourteen years, after Tristan was born. I could not run the restaurants and catering business effectively with a baby and no support. I would never be home. Tristan already had one parent he never saw; he didn't need two. Besides, I was completely burned out. I didn't think I could raise Tristan alone, and it wasn't fair to him. So I stayed, and Tom ignored the situation until the next time I brought it up.

As I sat at the long bar with Jack and Denise, we tried a flight of beer and looked around at the copper fermentation kettles. It was fascinating to see the operation and how organized it was. We greedily listened to the process from the distiller who was talking to us at the bar. We asked lots of questions while we settled in to taste the beer, all having a great time.

It was around ten thirty, and Jay had not shown up, so I figured he wasn't coming. Just as I leaned down to get something out of my purse, out of the corner of my eye, I saw him coming toward us. He had flowers in his hand and came up to me and handed them to me as he kissed me on the cheek.

"Happy birthday!" he said.

I was full of happiness at the sight of him. "Thank you, Jay! I'm so glad you could make it!"

"I almost didn't," Jay said, with a look of mild annoyance on his face.

"So this is the infamous Jay," Denise whispered to me after the introductions as we settled back into our seats at the bar. "He's cute."

I shushed her and turned back to Jay. "What do you mean, you almost didn't make it?" I asked him.

"Well, you said you would be at the Brew Pub. This is not the Brew Pub," he said like a teacher talking to a student who didn't finish her homework.

"It's not?" I asked. "Oops," I said, smiling and wrinkling my nose, a little thing I did that I knew he loved.

"Yeah, 'oops.' I had to ask three people directions to get here," he said, pretending to be annoyed, which he most likely was to some degree. "And it didn't help I didn't know the name of the place."

"I'm sorry. At least you are here now. Do you want to try a flight of beer?" I asked him. It was so good to see him, and we slipped right back into our roles.

"I think I'm going to take off," Jack said. It was around eleven, and Jack was studying to become a nurse. "I've got a ton of studying to do tomorrow and class in the morning."

Denise decided to leave as well. It was just Jay and I, alone again.

A little while later, I asked Jay, "Want to go out for breakfast? I'm hungry." It was a tradition to go out for breakfast after barhopping.

"Okay," Jay said.

We walked out to my car and climbed in. I was driving a Saab 900 at the time. I loved the car—the speed and the sound—and I thought it was cool that the ignition was on the floor between the two seats. It was also a stick shift, so it was a blast to drive.

As we headed toward the Massachusetts border on Route 195, it started to rain lightly. It was cold out, so the roads were slick. "Looks like black ice," I said to Jay as I slowed down.

Jay asked me about my marriage. He wanted to know whether I was happy or things were still strained between Tom and me.

"It hasn't changed much," I said. "But we are working through it."

I knew Jay could see right through me. He knew that our "working through it" meant I was doing most of the work and Tom wasn't satisfied.

I started to say something, but out of the corner of my eye, I saw a car coming up on us at a very high speed. It must have been going ninety miles an hour. The car hit a patch of ice and skidded toward us.

"Oh, my God!" I exclaimed.

The car hit the front left fender of my car with a loud thud. We immediately spun out of control.

"Oh, shit!" Jay said.

The rest was in slow motion. The car flipped over and landed on the roof and slid across the highway perpendicular to traffic as it continued to slowly spin while upside down. Finally, the car came to an abrupt stop as it hit the guardrail on the other side of the highway, crumpling both it and the car.

Jay's seat snapped in two, and he was thrown into the back seat. He was trapped and couldn't move.

I tried to remove my seat belt and saw my keychain dangling from what was now the ceiling of the car. I fumbled to get out, but the pressure of my weight pushing against it made it hard to unfasten.

"Are you okay, Carolyn?" he asked from the back seat, very worried.

"I think so. Are you?" I replied. My mind was whirling. I didn't know what to do, how to help Jay get out of the back seat. I was scared to death.

"Not really. I'm stuck and can't move. My heat is racing pretty fast." That was a big issue that worried us both; his father and brother had both died of a heart condition.

I saw that the driver-side window was smashed, and after I finally freed myself from my seat belt, I wiggled out of the window. The car was still on its roof, and I was afraid it might crumble. But it held steady.

The traffic was stopped around us, and off to the side of the road was a limousine that stopped to help. In it was a state trooper out for a night on the town, and I heard him yelling, "Where is the driver of this car?" as he pointed to my Saab. His friend was directing traffic, and I was wandering aimlessly on the highway, trying to get my bearings.

"I'm right here!" I yelled back at him when I collected my thoughts.

"Okay, is there anyone in the car?" he yelled back.

"Yes, his name is Jay," I replied. "He seems to be stuck in the back, and his heart is racing pretty fast. Please help him!"

He started to talk to Jay, calming him down while determining how he could free him from the back seat. I was talking to Jay from the open driver-side window. "How are you doing?" I asked.

The state trooper told me he had called 911 and that they would arrive momentarily. He asked me to get away from the car and went back to work trying to free Jay. He was worried it might catch fire. This made me very nervous.

I saw the man that had hit us; he was with his girlfriend standing in the middle of the highway. I stormed over toward him.

"What the hell were you thinking?" I screamed at him. "Why were you going so fast?" I was pissed; he had been going about thirty miles over the speed limit in a little blue Datsun 280Z, on black ice, no less. "Idiot Rhode Island driver!" I said to him. There was a reason Rhode Islanders had a reputation as terrible drivers, and here was a perfect example.

"I don't need this from you!" he screamed back. "I've had a really bad day!"

"You've had a bad day? You could have killed us!" I was furious. What a stupid thing to say. I walked away from him fuming and went back to check on the progress with Jay.

The ambulances, fire trucks, and police arrived, and Jay was extracted from the back seat, a feat that took almost an hour, and then we were each placed in an ambulance and taken to the emergency room at Rhode Island Hospital.

"You were really lucky," the paramedic said to me as he checked me over. "You only seem to have this one laceration. You will need stitches though."

"How is my friend?" I asked.

"He's on his way to the emergency room too. You will see him there," the paramedic answered; he was not about to give me any details.

While we were on the gurneys in the busy hospital emergency room, Jay asked one of the attendants whether I could be wheeled over to him. The attendant agreed, and in moments I was next to him.

"You okay?" he said to me, reaching out to hold my hand. As we both lay there on the gurneys, waiting for our turns with the emergency room doctors, we held hands in silence. I know we were both thinking about how lucky we were to have lived through the accident.

"Yes, I'm fine," I replied. "Is your heart still racing?" He was hooked up to a heart rate monitor, which was beeping away in the corner.

"Yes," he said with a worried look. "But they are watching me like a hawk. I'll be fine."

We stayed in the waiting area until finally we were taken into examination rooms. I ended up with a gash on my elbow that required five stitches. Hardly anything had happened to me. Jay's heart stopped racing, and he was instructed to take it easy for a couple of days and follow up with his cardiologist to make sure everything was okay.

It was about three thirty in the morning when Jay was released. He didn't want to leave me, but I wanted him to go home and rest. He said he was going to take a cab back to his car. "What's the name of that pub we were at again?" Jay asked. We both smiled at the joke. "We were pretty fortunate tonight," he said to me seriously. He watched while the doctor checked me over and stitched me up.

"I know," I agreed. "That could have been much worse." I was tired, upset, and worried. Worried about Jay, worried how we were going to get home, worried about how I was going to explain this to Tom.

"How are you going to get home?" he asked.

"I'll call a cab as well," I said.

"I won't leave you. I need to see you home," Jay replied. Ever the gentleman.

"No, you go home and rest. I'll be fine," I said. I was already wondering how I was going to explain this to Tom; having Jay escort me home would only add fuel to the fire.

"Are you sure?" he said.

"Yes, please go. I won't be much longer here anyway," I said to him.

Jay kissed me on the cheek and reluctantly began to leave. "Take care of yourself," he said.

"Bye, Jay," I called out to him softly. "Thanks for spending my birthday with me. I'm so sorry about all this."

He turned around and smiled at me gently.

When I was finally released from the hospital, it was about five o'clock, and the sun was beginning to come up. I called a cab and rode home, wondering how I was going to handle this explanation to Tom. I was dreading the conversation but knew I had to tell him.

The cab pulled up in front of our home, and I got out and slowly walked up the steps to the porch. I was stiff and sore. Tom was watching from the window and opened the door as I approached.

"Where have you been?" he asked, looking very worried. For all the unhappiness we had in our marriage, I think Tom did love me, as much as he could have. Tempered love. Conditional love.

"I was in an accident. The car flipped over on 195, black ice. But I'm okay," I reported.

"I was worried. Why didn't you call?" he asked. "Are you all right?"

"I was in the emergency room. I couldn't. And I'm fine, just a few stitches," I replied as I pulled up the sleeve of my thick Álafoss sweater to show him. The sweater had bloodstains on it, and in the ambulance, the paramedic had wanted to cut it off me. I wouldn't let him; I loved that sweater. "Do you mind if I go to bed? I really need to get some sleep."

He looked at me and said, "No, go ahead."

Around eleven that morning, the phone rang. It felt like the middle of the night; I had been asleep only a few hours and was groggy when I heard Tom pick up the receiver and say hello. This was followed by silence. I bolted out of bed; it couldn't have been good news. They had taken my car to the junkyard, and I thought it might be the police.

As I walked into the living room, Tom handed the phone to me and said, "It's Jay." He was not happy.

I covered the receiver and said to Tom, "I was going to talk to you about this when I got up. Jay came down to wish me a happy birthday last night. He was in the car when we flipped over."

Tom just looked at me and said, "You deceived me." Then he stormed off into the kitchen. He never said another word about it, and I was terrified to bring it up.

Tom knew all about Jay and the relationship we had before Tom and I were married. He never wanted to talk about it, but he did notice and grumble something under his breath when Jay called on holidays and birthdays, completely not understanding why Jay would do such a thing. Once when I was looking through some old boxes, I came across an empty plastic container that had once held the beautiful photographs Alice had taken of Jay and me, along with his letters and cards to me. I had packed them up and stored them away. Tom found them and decided to throw them out, so that was the end of that.

"How are you feeling today?" Jay asked me after I said hello.

"I'm sore," I said. "How about you?"

"The same," he replied.

"What time did you finally get home?" I asked him.

"Around five thirty. I got a cab back to my car and drove home," Jay replied.

I was upset that Jay had called me before I had gotten a chance to talk to Tom about what happened the night before. It seemed as if Jay always called me when he knew Tom would be home, just to let him know he was still around.

"Did you tell me once you have a friend that is a lawyer?" he asked.

"Yes, Linda is a lawyer and a great friend," I replied.

"Can I have her number?" he requested.

"Sure, I'll have her call you. I don't have it with me right now," I replied.

"Okay, thanks. Well, I just wanted to check in on you. I'm glad you are all right," Jay said. "I hope you are not in too much trouble with Tom." I couldn't tell whether he was being sarcastic or was truly worried about it. Jay didn't like the way Tom treated me, and Tom ignored any situation involving Jay. There was no love lost between the two of them; that was for sure.

"Me too," I replied; my guilt was almost unbearable. We said good-bye.

As I hung up the phone, Tom came back in from the kitchen, wanting to know all the details about the accident. "I have to figure out what to do about your car," he said. This was most important in this situation to him; everything else he would have to ignore so we wouldn't have to talk about it.

22

GET THE HELL AWAY FROM ME

Tom was on the road, and it was just Tristan and I. I loved our time together; he was such a fun little kid to be around. We spent the weeks exploring and having fun after nursery school let out each day at eleven thirty.

"Daddy will be home tonight!" I said to Tristan.

"Goody!" His adorable little face lit up at the news.

"Maybe you can stay up late and see him. Give him a big hug..." I said, kneeling down to be eye level. The thought of staying up was exciting to the little one. "We can make popcorn and watch *One Hundred One Dalmatians!*"

He threw his arms around me and said, "Yay!"

Later that night we could hear Tom coming home. The car door slammed, and he was getting his luggage out of the trunk of the car.

"Let's hide and surprise him!" I said to Tristan.

We jumped up from the couch, where we were snuggling with the dog, blankets, and a bowl of popcorn. We hid behind the closet door, peeking out as we waited for him. Tristan giggled and put his chubby little finger up to his mouth and said, "Shhh!"

Tom opened the door and walked into the living room. "Goddamn dog!" he said loudly when the dog happily ran up to greet him. "Get the hell away from me!" he sneered as he pushed the dog out of the way with his foot, a little too harshly. This was becoming the ritual by which he announced his arrival. I was thinking that this was how he seemed to feel about me as well. As Tristan watched the scene, my heart went out to him. He looked so sad as the smile left his face. I could feel the happiness drain from the room.

Tristan recovered quickly, and he jumped out from behind the door and yelled, "Surprise, Daddy!" He was so cute. I just couldn't get enough of him.

Tom dropped one of his suitcases and said, "What do we have here?" Tristan ran up to him and hugged his leg. Tom patted him on the back awkwardly. Tristan scurried off to get back to the movie and popcorn.

I walked over to Tom to hug him, and he responded with a half hug, patting me on the back with about as much emotion as a robot, while still holding his suitcase.

"Give me a real hug!" I said to him, smiling. He put down his suitcase and wrapped both arms around me, squeezing tightly—much too tightly. He wasn't trying to be kind and tender; this hug was meant to show me who was boss.

Later, after we tucked Tristan into bed, I said to him, "I can't understand how anyone can hate dogs so much..." I said. "They are warm and happy, love you unconditionally, and just want to please you. How can that be a bad thing?" Even as I was saying it, I knew that Tom did not understand unconditional love at all. It didn't make sense to him.

"They are just stupid animals," he said.

I just sighed lightly and said, "I'm going to bed."

"Good night. I'm going to go through the mail," he replied. "See you in the morning."

23

TWENTY-SIX MILES TODAY

I was waiting for Jay in his apartment. The key was left in the usual place, and I let myself in. I was feeling an undeniable guilt for being there. As hollow and unhappy as I felt, I was still married. "I will not sleep with him," I told myself with conviction. I knew the offer would be there, but I wouldn't do it. I probably shouldn't have even come to visit, but I did want to see whether he was okay after his surgery.

I looked around his apartment. It was big—too big for one person, I always thought. Ten rooms, four bedrooms, pantry, kitchen, dining room, curved staircase to the first-floor entry—it had so much potential. At this point, it was a bachelor pad—with more reading material than anyone possibly needed. "What would I do with this place if I could get my hands on it?" I thought. "Well, first thing I would do is clean it up and paint it prettier colors…"

Jay came in from his ride, clamoring up the flights of stairs with his bike.

"Twenty-six miles today!" he stated proudly.

"Good for you!" I said, impressed. "Where did you end up going?

"Brookline, Brighton, Watertown," Jay replied. "The doctor told me after my surgery that if I didn't get my heart rate up and exercise regularly, I would be back in the hospital for another surgery soon enough."

"Well, I'm glad you are listening," I said, smiling at him. I handed him a small bouquet of get-well flowers.

He seemed to be doing very well.

"Thank you. Your turn this time?" he said, laughing. "Nice little role reversal there."

"I thought you might appreciate getting them for a change," I said, smiling.

"It's great to see you, Carolyn. What's up?" he asked, looking at me intently.

"I just wanted to see you, say hello, see how you were after your surgery," I replied.

"Well, thank you. That's nice of you to check up on me," he said.

I was thinking about years before, when I was sick with the flu. He had driven over an hour one night after he got out of work to bring me chicken soup. He heated it and spoon-fed me while I was in bed. When I asked him why he had gone to so much trouble, he replied, "It's good for you. You're sick, and I want to take care of you. Besides, chicken soup cures all. It's Jewish penicillin." He was thoughtful that way.

"You must be hungry. Want to grab something?" I asked.

"I am," Jay said. "Let's go out. Chinese food?" He loved Chinese food.

"Okay, but can you have that after your surgery?" I asked. Jay was exercising so intensely because he had gone through bypass surgery just weeks before. He upped his game and was eating right and exercising like a madman.

Jay put up his index finger and said, "Yes. As long as I'm careful. Shrimp good. Lobster bad." Then he opened the refrigerator and pulled out a bottle of juice and drank deeply.

"Okay," I said. "Whenever you're ready."

"I need to take a shower first," he said. "Care to join me?" he said and pulled me toward him and wrapped his arms around me.

"Jay, I can't," I said, pulling away from him.

"Why not?" he replied. "I haven't seen you in a long time. I've missed you."

My mind wandered as we stood there together. I knew exactly what he wanted: the same thing as always. There was no denying the passion between us. I loved being in his warm embrace, my head resting on his heart. And making love with him was incredible. He showed me things about my own body I didn't even know existed. I thought back on something he used to say to me: "You're every man's dream, a perfect lady until you turn into a tigress in the bedroom. I'm a very lucky man." Jay loved the fact I was the all-American girl. What he loved most was that this particular all-American girl couldn't get enough of him in bed. But that was over.

I shook my head to bring myself back to reality and to get the scenes of our passion out of my mind. It had been a long time ago.

"'Missed' me?" I said, getting back on track. "Those days are over."

"I will always want you. You're beautiful," he replied.

Now I knew he was giving me a line of BS. I was a lot bigger than the last time he saw me; I had had a baby, and it showed on my hips, and pretty much everywhere else. But this didn't seem to stop him from kissing me. Again, I pulled away.

"I just came up to see you to make sure you were okay after your surgery. I just wanted to say hello, not pick up where we left off," I said to him.

"Well, I appreciate that. I was wondering whether I was going to make it," Jay said as he pulled away from me. He knew it was a lost cause.

I hadn't realized it was so serious. I shot him with a quizzical look.

"Yeah," he said, "the doctor told me I better smarten up or it would be the end of me. As it is, I may have to go back into surgery, this time for a triple bypass."

"Oh, man, I'm so sorry. I didn't realize it was that bad," I said to him sadly.

"How would you know? It's been a while," he replied, looking at me.

"Yes, I guess so," I said back to him.

"Know what I'm going to do?" he asked me.

"What?" I replied.

"I'm going to marry you some day," he stated with conviction.

That idea seemed to come out of nowhere. "Oh, really?" I replied with little emotion. It was a nice thought, but I wasn't going to hold my breath.

"Yes, when you get back down to your fighting weight," he said. "Then you will be happy, and we can be together."

"Okay, well, we'll see," I responded. That smarted. So I had to lose weight to be happy? Says who? Not only was I hurt, but I was pissed.

As I thought about his message to me, I realized he was very serious about this exercise routine, getting in shape, and living a healthier lifestyle. He obviously wanted me to be healthier as well. He had never been that way before. I guess when you are facing death, you look at things differently.

He came closer to me again and embraced me in a hug, leaning down to kiss me. "Come on. Let's go into the bedroom," he pleaded.

"No," I said firmly. If I was too overweight to marry, I was certainly too overweight to sleep with. "I've got to go, and I'm glad you are okay," I said as I put my coat on and gathered my purse and keys to leave.

He looked deflated. "Okay," he said, raising his hands in defeat.

"Take care of yourself," I said and walked down the stairs and out to my car. He watched from the window as I pulled away from the curb.

24

FLY ME TO THE MOON

I was working in the kitchen, creating a Sunday dinner with my earphones on, singing at the top of my lungs. We were having a dinner party, and I wanted to show my friends how much I appreciated them by making a wonderful dinner. I was alone in the house and was taking advantage of the solitude to let loose and be myself.

"Fly me to the moon!" I belted out. "Let me play among the stars!" I continued blissfully in my best Frank Sinatra imitation. "Let me see what spring is like on Jupiter and Mars. In other words, hold my hand." I was on a roll now. "In other words, pleeease be true! In other words, I love you!"

I was running around the kitchen, rinsing red potatoes and making a fresh garlic butter to roast them in. I was in my glory. Cooking and music—the two things that put me in a state of pure bliss.

As I bent down toward the oven to check the roast, I noticed that Tom had walked into the room. He was angry, as usual. "Will you take those stupid things off?" he snarled as he put down the bags he was carrying, making a gesture with his hands as though he were pulling something off his ears.

"Sorry, what?" I said, removing the earphones.

"Take those damn things off. You're too loud!" he replied irritably.

Now granted, I was too loud, and I couldn't sing, but I was alone in the house, and he wasn't due back for another hour or so. I thought it was safe, as everyone was out of earshot of my harmonic howling.

"Okay, okay," I said. "Sorry." I felt completely deflated. There was such contempt in his eyes. I didn't know whether he was mad at me for being too loud or for enjoying myself so much. It could have been either, but I suspected it was the latter. I put the earphones back in their case and put them away.

"Thank you," he said, exasperated. "So what is the schedule for today?" he asked.

"We went over this yesterday, twice. Why did you need to interrupt me while I was in my happy place to ask me that?" I asked. Now I was getting irritable.

"No one wants to hear you sing, and you're waking up the dead," he said, trying to be funny. He wasn't. He had a terrible sense of humor and was the worst ever at telling a joke.

Tommie was rigid and organized and needed to know what the upcoming plans were at all times. He had a way of holding information hostage. Once he found out what he wanted to know, he was completely done with our conversation, and usually me. Once he had collected the information needed, he could set up his plan of attack for the day. Tom was all about tasks, schedules, and plans. We were never allowed to veer off those plans, or all hell would break loose, and we would all have to pay for it and deal with his sulking.

Every morning when he was not traveling, he would wake up and want to know what I was doing and when, even before I had a cup of coffee and shook off the cobwebs from sleep.

"So what are your plans for today?" he would ask.

"Give me a minute to wake up!" I would reply, completely exasperated. It was getting old day after day, but I realized if I withheld information from him, he would pay attention to me. It was a twisted way of communicating, but I learned how to do it pretty well. It's just how our marriage and our communication worked.

25

THE CHOICES WE MAKE

Later that week we met Linda and Kim for dinner in Providence. "I'm glad you and Tommie were able to meet us tonight," Linda said to me as we fixed our makeup in the bathroom mirror of the restaurant.

"So am I," I said. "It's been way too long. Kim seems great, by the way." Kim was Linda's husband.

"He is great, happy at his new job," she said, smiling. "I have something I wanted to talk with you about in private."

Linda was, first, one of my closest friends and, second, my lawyer. We hadn't seen each other for a while; our lives seemed to be on autopilot. I knew something was up when she asked us out to dinner so abruptly. Linda was kind and loving and brilliant. I loved having her as a friend.

"I talked to Jay this week," she continued.

"Oh?" I said as I dabbed lipstick on in the mirror. This was not what I was expecting. I was still not happy that the last words he had said to me were "I'm going to marry you some day," followed by something about my weight. I hadn't talked to him in over two years. It just seemed simpler that way.

"What did he have to say?" I asked. Linda was Jay's attorney too, and they had become friends after she represented him after the accident on my birthday years before.

"Well," Linda began. "He is going back into the hospital for another bypass surgery," she said seriously, searching my face for clues as to how I felt about this piece of news.

I didn't know how to relate to this bit of information. I was numb. When I was younger, I wanted so much to marry Jay, to be with him for life, but he wanted to find his fame and fortune in the world, and there was no place in it for me.

"Oh, no. Really? When?" I asked as I continued to look into the mirror. For some reason, I just couldn't bear to look at Linda directly.

"Next week," she said. "He wanted me to tell you he's not sure he is going to make it this time."

I finally pulled my eyes off myself in the mirror and stared at her as she continued.

"The doctors are not sure he is strong enough."

"I don't know what to say," I replied. Jay had been part of my life for so long, even if only on the sidelines lately. Linda knew our entire story and had been with me as a sounding board for much of it. She never judged. I felt blessed to have such a good friend.

"It's okay. He just wanted you to know. He didn't want to interrupt your life with Tommie and Tristan again. He knows you're happy, that you made your choice."

I was happy, as happy as I could be in a union without love. My bright spot in all this was that I adored being a mother. Tristan was my life, and motherhood agreed with me.

"I'm not sure the choice was mine to make, Linda," I responded.

She smiled at me knowingly.

"You know I loved him so much..." I continued.

"I know," she said.

"He's the one who wanted to follow his passion, go to California, find his way in acting," I continued.

"Yes, I remember," she said.

"So how was it my choice?" I said. "Sometimes I think that if I could have Jay with Tommie's circumstances, I would have the perfect man for me."

"What do you mean?" Linda asked.

"Well, the love, passion, and kindness of Jay. His creativity, his talent, his intellect, his spontaneity. I loved being around him. We were so good together, and I adored him."

"I know you did. The feeling was mutual," Linda said gently.

"And the stability of Tommie, the children..." I continued. "You know, he was the type of man I was supposed to marry. Stable, solid, successful. If I could only have put the two of them together, meld them somehow." I realized it was futile, but the thought had crossed my mind more than once.

Linda said as she chuckled softly, "But that didn't work out, did it?"

"No, it didn't," I said. "You know I would go running back to Jay if he stepped up to the plate."

"I know you would, but you have Tristan," she replied.

"Which is exactly why I stay with Tommie. I do love him in my own way. He's good to us and can be a good father when he wants to be."

"Yes, I can see that," Linda said.

I went on. "But there is absolutely no spark, no passion, no laughter."

"You two seem good together though," Linda said, although she knew all too well that I was depressed and it was getting worse.

"I'm glad it appears that way. But it's lonely. Tommie's gone from Sunday afternoon till midnight on Friday, traveling. I have asked him to try to find a position where he can be home, but he just doesn't want to. He says he can't, but he doesn't try either. I think he likes having a part-time family. The only problem is I'm the one who has to dry Tristan's tears when he wakes up crying for his father at night."

"Yes, he does talk about his frequent flyer miles a lot," Linda said, giggling. "And don't get him going about the airlines!"

"Yes, that and he loves to have his *US Today* delivered to his door every morning at the hotel, where everyone is waiting on him hand and foot. 'Yes, sir. Of course, sir.' I think he resents the fact that he comes home and I tell him the trash needs to go out," I explained.

"Come on, Carolyn, is it really that bad?" Linda laughed as she responded to my mini tirade. I was definitely in drama-queen mode.

"No, I guess not. But it isn't the life I thought I wanted either," I replied.

Linda came over to me and gave me a hug. "I'm sorry," she said.

"No, I'm sorry. You came to me with something important to say, and I'm feeling sorry for myself. What else about Jay?" I asked.

"Nothing really. He's just scared and wanted you to know what was happening and that he was thinking about you," she said.

"Maybe I should talk with him." As soon as the words came out of my mouth, I knew I would never do it. The thought of talking to him at this point was frightening. Profess my undying love for him while he was on his deathbed? How dramatic, and at this point I didn't think I felt it anymore. What good would that do? He had turned me away a few times. I had to concentrate on my family and do what I could to create a happy life for us.

"That's up to you, dear. Do what feels right in your heart," Linda responded.

"I know. I'll think about it," I said. The problem was I didn't know what was in my heart anymore.

26

STURDY LEGS

It was a cool autumn evening, and after we grilled some steaks and had a salad with bread I had baked earlier, Tom's family and I were outside, sitting by a crackling fire. We were drinking warm cider with spiced rum, a touch of red currant, and a cinnamon stick. I was sitting with my sisters-in-law, who were talking about some neighbor or another that bought a new car. I was completely bored with the conversation.

Tom's family loved to gossip and talk about current events, TV, clothes, and other subjects that didn't seem to matter much to me. They thought they were being kind or even refined about it by saying things like "It's too bad about this" or "Did you hear about such-and-such? It's sad," but still, it was gossip. One thing I learned being part of this family was that you did not talk about your feelings, your ideas, or anything philosophical, deep, interesting, or, heaven forbid, spiritual. I yearned to talk about spirituality, something I was always interested in, but whenever I brought it up, I was usually met with a blank stare. They were very frustrating to have a conversation with. I remember one evening Tom's parents received an invitation to the wedding of an old neighbor who was getting married to a young man who came from a wealthy family. Tom's sisters spent quite awhile examining and discussing the invitation, putting it up to the light, getting a magnifying glass—trying to determine whether the invitation was engraved. I watched in horrified amazement. Who the hell cared? What difference did it make? They were missing the whole point of what was important—someone they grew up with was getting married. A cause for celebration!

At times like these, I would go for a walk or ask Tristan whether he wanted to play a game or play cards. Focusing my attention elsewhere was how I held my tongue and made it through the family gatherings.

One of my favorite quotes by Eleanor Roosevelt popped into my head as we sat there: "Great minds discuss ideas; average minds discuss events; small minds discuss people." It was obvious which categories this family fit in to.

Tom and his brother-in-law Fred were standing a few feet away, talking about Fred's recent trip to Saint Kitts, where he had gone with friends, and without his wife. "You should have seen her. She had legs up to her neck! But of course, what happens on the island stays on the island," Fred said to Tom, laughing. Tom laughed, but I knew he didn't really think it was funny. He wasn't sure, be it did cross his mind that Fred was cheating on his sister and telling him about it. The family put up with it because it was easier to ignore, than bring it up and deal with it.

"Well, good for you. Imagine what it's like to have to live with my wife's legs! They are like cement blocks and could hold up the Empire State Building," I heard Tom say to Fred.

I whipped my head around, not believing what I had heard. Tom and Fred were laughing.

"Oooh, I think you went too far that time," Fred said to Tom in a warning tone, still laughing. I was crushed and completely embarrassed. Of all the things my husband could say about me, he chose to make fun of my "sturdy legs," as he called them. They were big. So what? That didn't define me. My up-and-down weight was something I had been struggling with and been ashamed of my entire life. I didn't care whether he had had one too many drinks; saying something like that, knowing it was a struggle, was just plain mean. It was even worse that he said it in front of his perfect little family of "beautiful people," the ones with the great legs.

"That was just mean. Go to hell!" I said to Tom angrily. My sisters-in-law were looking at me, one trying to hide a smile, the other ignoring the situation.

Tom was still standing there with Fred, laughing and looking proud of himself. Score one for the men. They reminded me of stuck-up little frat boys collecting yet another story of someone's shortcomings or embarrassment for them to share at dinner parties.

I stood up and quickly walked into the house, trying to keep my composure and act as if it didn't bother me. Showing emotions was frowned on in this family; it was a sign of weakness. I could feel the sting of tears in my eyes, but I didn't want them to see me upset. Tom stood there, watching me walk by, and didn't follow me or say a word. He didn't seem to care much, or at least couldn't let his family think he did.

Tom's idea of being funny was to point out my flaws, both physical and mental. He always seemed to know how to pinpoint my soft spots and dig.

27

GONE

The phone jangled loudly, and I ran to pick it up. It was Linda. "Hello, beautiful!" I said happily, but my gut told me it was not good news.

"I just got a call from Jay's brother Marc. Jay didn't make it," she said gently.

My heart sank. Every hope I had for a happy life with this man was gone with this simple message. I hadn't realized it would hit me so hard. Thoughts and memories of us being together—our conversations, his kindness, his caring, walking along the beach, kissing under the stars, laughing with friends, making love—all came rushing back to me.

"Oh, dear," I said sadly. I had no idea what else to say. I felt numb. "Can I do anything?" I asked, trying to fill the silence.

"No, everything is taken care of. As you know, Marc is in the Middle East and asked me to get things squared away here for him. His mother is in Israel, and they are meeting there for a funeral."

Jay's mother had lived in Israel for as long as I had known Jay. I never had the chance to meet her, but I understand she was strong and funny. I think I would have liked her a lot. The family raised the kids in Brooklyn until his father passed, and his mother wanted to be with her family so moved to Israel.

"Thanks, Linda. I appreciate your letting me know," I said softly.

"If you need to talk, I'm here," she replied.

"Thank you," I said with a huge lump in my throat, trying my best to get off the phone with some trace of composure before I could let the tears loose.

I hung up the phone and went into the living room, flopped down on the couch, and cried into the pillows for a good long time. The sun had set, and rain started pelting the windows as it grew dark. I fell asleep and woke as I heard Tom come home from taking Tristan out for a haircut and Saturday errands.

"What's the matter now?" Tommie asked, standing next to the couch. It was obvious I had been crying. He wanted to know what the matter was, not necessarily to comfort me but more for information-gathering purposes. He definitely didn't want to get into a discussion about the reason I was crying yet again.

"Nothing, I'm fine," I said, secretly wishing he would put his arm around me, comfort me somehow. Maybe hold my hand. That was just not the way he did things. Showing emotion of any kind was hard, almost impossible for him. But I yearned for a tender touch, a kind word, a hug.

"No, you're not. Now tell me what's the matter," he said, losing patience.

"Jay died," I said softly.

"Oh," he said. And that was that. Tommie got up and walked out of the room. I knew he wasn't happy with me for being so sad about Jay's death. Tommie knew all about Jay; he knew I dated him for a long time before we met and that I still had some feelings for him. Jay would call to check in, and Tom would answer the phone and say, "It's some guy named Jay," and hand the phone to me. It was uncomfortable, and I think Jay sometimes called just to let Tommie know he was still around.

It's not that I thought Jay and I would have walked off into the sunset together; it was too late for that. Our lives and what we wanted out of life were too different. At this point, I knew that any bit of happiness with love I might have had just died with Jay.

28

ONE LAST TWIST OF THE KNIFE

Over the next several years, we went about our lives. We moved to the mountain region of New Hampshire and then near the seacoast as Tristan grew up. I was so happy and in love with my life as a mother. Things were good for a while on the marriage front. Although Tom and I didn't have a crazy-in-love relationship, it was comfortable, and we got along for the most part. It wasn't so bad. I learned to live with it.

One May we decided to take the family on a trip to Europe and were staying in a little hotel in London, near Paddington Station. I was visiting my cousin and gallivanting around the countryside as well as taking in the sights, sounds, and incredible history of the city. We had a wonderful time, and it was a nice respite from the day-to-day routine of home. The only damper on the trip was that my mother was ill. Just the week before, after years of avoiding it, she had finally asked me to take her to the doctor, who then referred her to an oncologist. She had about two months to live. Her liver was enlarged, her skin was gray, and we found out that she had lung cancer that had metastasized into her bones.

She didn't make it even two weeks. I saw a missed call from the 716 area code and listened to the message on my cell phone. It was my brother, and I knew it had to be bad news. Mom had died. I didn't feel sadness, just relief. That said a lot about our relationship. She was my mother, but I just didn't seem to have any more tears left in me to shed over our relationship.

The funeral was going to be two days after we got back from London, and Greg said he would take care of the arrangements. "Great, about time he stepped up to the plate," I thought. I could be a real bitch when I wanted to be.

We were sitting in the funeral home during the wake. I hadn't seen my brother in about eight years. He wasn't allowed to see his family, and he made no effort to fight his wife, Ellie, about it, as far as I could tell.

As I sat in a chair facing the casket, I was thinking about the relationship I had with my mother, and I was finding it hard to grieve. I did my best to show the obligatory remorse and sadness but I wasn't feeling it.

A few people were milling around and talking. Greg came down to sit beside me, and he leaned over and said, "I just wanted to let you know Mom didn't leave you anything." He was pretending to be sad. I was being handled. I'm sure he chose to tell me this bit of news with other people around so he didn't have to face me alone, or so I didn't make a scene, which I never would have. This man didn't know me at all. I think he thought this was a good way to keep me under control. He could be such a jerk.

I looked at him and said, "Hmmm, no surprise there."

"Yeah, sorry about that," he said. No emotion, no feeling. I looked at him with a blank stare. What did he want me to say?

I had known this little bombshell was coming since before she died. One day years earlier, after my father died, I was going through some old pictures of the family to see which ones I could frame and display on the family wall of photos at home. I came across her last will and testament in the back of the desk. There it was, in pretty-plain legalese, that I was disowned, everything was left to my brother, and I was to have nothing. "One last twist of the knife," I thought as I read it. I wasn't mad, just hurt and resigned to the fact that any illusions I had of us being a happy family were futile. At least one good thing came of it: all the guilt I placed on myself for her not loving me vanished.

After the funeral, I planned to meet my brother back at my mother's house to help him clean out the junk that had accumulated over the years. My brother had offered me my mother's eight-year-old car earlier that day because he thought there might be some value in it. I wasn't really sure what to make of that offer.

As I entered my mother's house, I noticed everything of value, everything that was nice, expensive, or worth anything, was gone—packed up in a truck and ready to head back to western New York. What was left were a few broken and tattered pieces of old furniture, old kitchen utensils, and my parents' personal belongings from the bureaus. I didn't really care about all the stuff. The only thing I had ever asked my mother to leave me was an engagement and wedding ring that she had inherited from my favorite aunt. That aunt had meant a lot to me and was like a grandmother to me when I was a child. It had a lot of sentimental meaning. I realized that it was not something I was going to have when after the funeral service, the funeral director gave my brother my mother's personal effects and the jewelry she was wearing, which he slipped into his suit-jacket pocket. Later, when I saw his wife, Ellie, she was wearing the ring, having removed her own. This woman couldn't stand my mother but certainly didn't mind wearing her three-carat diamond ring.

As I walked into the house, my brother said, "Hi. We are almost done going through all this stuff. We have everything we want, and if you want anything that is left over, go ahead and take it."

"Thank you, Greg," I said to my brother with a bit of sarcasm, looking around at the unwanted old furniture, kitchen dishes, and piles of junk ready to be discarded. The sarcasm was lost on him.

I went to the back of the house and started to go through my father's dresser drawers. My father had died ten years before, and nothing in his dresser had ever been touched. This was where the things that were really valuable to me were. In the bottom drawer, I found old 78 records and films of the few family vacations we had been on. I also found pictures of the family growing up and of my grandparents, aunts, and uncles, along with people I didn't know in World War II uniforms. There were pictures of my father and me, which brought a smile to my face. I missed him so much. His father was a cobbler, and they moved to the States from Carlisle, England, to start a new life. My father was kind and caring and loved me very much, even if he was not able to show it. My mother didn't like the competition.

As I was going through the bureau, I thought back on our one fun vacation so many years earlier and began looking for the pictures to show Greg. We didn't do much as a family, but I thought it would be nice to have pictures of the one good holiday we did have. I found them in a box in the bottom drawer, and I walked outside to find Greg with a few pictures I wanted to show him of the two of us when we were younger. I found him near the Dumpster in our driveway, talking to Terri, who was going through stuff he was ready to discard, looking for treasures.

"Look, isn't this adorable?" I asked him happily. "It's us as little kids! Remember this vacation? We were so cute!" I beamed as I showed him the picture. "That was a fun trip, wasn't it?"

"Oh, yeah, that's nice," he said with a fake smile, barely glancing at the picture.

I continued. "I found all these great family pictures. Which ones do you want me to save for you? I thought we could divvy them up."

"Why would I want those?" he asked me. I thought I saw a fleeting look of disgust on his face but wasn't sure.

I looked at him in surprise, feeling hurt that he wanted absolutely no mementos of our life together as kids. "Okay, I just thought that you may want some of them. Maybe frame one or two of them to remind you that you have a family too." It was a snarky thing to say, but the events of the past few days were wearing thin, and I was losing my patience.

"Nope, not interested. I don't know what I'd do with them," he said, pretending he didn't hear the last part of what I had just said to him.

Walking away, I wasn't exactly sure why he would *need* them as opposed to *want* them. So I buried that feeling a little deeper and went back into the house.

Years later I heard through the family grapevine that an uncle of ours had visited Greg and his family in Buffalo and was surprised and hurt to see that there was not one single picture of our side of the family anywhere to be found in the house. It was as if our family simply didn't exist. Plenty of pictures of Ellie's family, though.

Over the next couple of days, I helped my brother clean out the house and get it ready to sell. Ellie had gone back home to Buffalo, and he stayed behind, finishing up the dirty work.

After we said our good-byes and Greg headed for home, I wrote him a letter. I wanted him to know that I was not upset about the will and how things turned out and that I wouldn't do anything to make his life miserable about it. I just wanted us to be a happy family and stay connected. I also wanted him to know that if I could do anything to help him or his family, I would be there for him. He wasn't much of a brother, but he was all I had, and at this point I was alone as far as family was concerned. I was hoping we could have open lines of communication, at least. He never replied.

29

BOUNCING AROUND

After years in New Hampshire, we decided to move to Charleston, South Carolina, after hitting financial strain during the housing crisis. I had changed careers from chef and restaurateur to real estate broker, and it proved to be very successful for me. I ended up becoming the top-producing agent in our office within a year of receiving my license and decided to purchase the office I worked for. I grew the office to around forty agents, received my principal broker's license, and purchased a farmhouse built in 1872, rehabbing it from top to bottom to bring it back to its previous glory. I enjoyed every minute of re-creating this space, but it proved to be very bad timing.

I considered the financial issues we faced as a family to be entirely my fault. The company I built grew too fast, and I believed the real estate boom would continue for a long time to come. For many years, we lived an empty but fun life of abundance, parties, friends, vacation homes, rental property, worldwide travel, and lots of "things." Tom and I had learned how to get along well enough, and the success in business certainly seemed to help. But we were happy on the outside, hollow on the inside. When the housing crisis hit, the business closed its doors in less than a year. Tom stood by me as we went through the mess of selling off—or losing, I should say—four houses and much of the contents of each.

It was hard on the family, but we were strong and muddled through with dignity and a sense of purpose. We did our best to pay off whatever debt we could, but there came a point when the well ran dry. Looking back, I see it was the best thing that could have happened to us. It woke us up to what and who was important in our lives.

After things settled down, we discussed what the next phase of our life should be, what challenge we would tackle next. Tristan was done with high school and would be going off to college. We made the decision to move to Charleston, South Carolina. We both loved the South: the history, the architecture, the people, the incredible food, the weather—everything about it. So we packed up our things and headed south.

We were living comfortably in Mount Pleasant, which was just over the Ravenel Bridge from Charleston. We had many friends there and enjoyed our lives. By this point, we had another child, Sam, who was many years younger than Tristan. Once again, I loved being a mother and having another little one to take care of.

We spent four very happy years there until one day Tom announced that the company he worked for was closing and he had to find a new position.

Late one afternoon just after he told me about the company closing, we were discussing the situation while sitting outside, sipping cocktails, and enjoying the soft sunshine. I asked Tom whether he thought we should move back to Rhode Island, since he was making changes in his position and it might be a good time. I wanted to be closer to Tristan, and I had to admit, even though they drove me nuts half the time, I missed his family. It was all the family I had, and I craved the connection.

"Your mom is failing, and maybe it would be a good thing to move back to help take care of her," I said to Tom.

"Maybe," Tom said, but I knew he liked the idea. So that was that. I was off and running to find a way to make that happen.

It was also time for me to look for a traditional job. I wanted to contribute more to the family. Within three weeks I had been offered a position as CEO of a real estate brokerage in New England, and three weeks after that, we were on the road, moving back. Tom also found a position easily, mostly because he would travel anywhere, so we were headed back home. I was amazed at how easily everything fell into place and how quickly it all happened. It was almost too fast and too easy. It seemed to be guided in some way.

30

BACK TO RHODY

After we moved back to Rhode Island, we easily got back into the New England pace of things. One evening, when we were stressed and overtaxed from the move, I complained about something Tom considered stupid, and we began arguing. I was tired and grumpy and just wanted to rest. The need for rest was considered a weakness by Tom, so he was frustrated with me yet again. Something hit Tom on a deep level, and he exploded.

"I have given you everything!" he screamed at me. "Why can't you just do what I want you to do?" I didn't have any idea what had brought this on, but I knew what he meant. It meant that he had worked hard all his life to give me things. Things I didn't necessarily want or need, but he was being a good husband in his mind. I know I wasn't that easy to live with either, but everything in our world was caught up in current events, who did what to whom, who drove what, what they were doing—stuff that didn't amount to much of anything in the big picture. It was frustrating to me to live on such a superficial level. If I tried a bit harder, maybe I could help him understand what was truly important, the giving of oneself to another. Unconditional love.

"I have given you me!" I shouted back. It was hard for me to understand why Tom didn't realize this. He became silent. A quizzical look came across his face as though something had dawned on him. He didn't seem to be able to muster a response. I thought giving myself to Tom would prove to be a good thing, and that he would reciprocate, at least to some degree. If I showed him love and kindness in our life together, he would begin to understand, maybe even participate on a deeper level. It was wishful thinking.

The next day at work, one of the agents in the office asked me whether I would like to see a medium and psychic that she had been going to for years. I thought it would be fun and agreed. Her name was April, and this appointment turned out to be the beginning of a phase in my life I could not even have begun to imagine.

31

FIRST READING, CONTINUED

"Okay, let's keep going," April said. "He is saying that he knew you were not living the life you were meant to, because when he went through his life review on the other side, he found out that you were supposed to go on and build a family, and he was supposed to go on and build his career. Later the two of you would have gotten back together. That was your destiny."

"Oh, wow," I said, mesmerized. How do you come up with a response for something like that? I was hard pressed to think of anything more than "Oh, wow."

April continued. "He's saying that he lost faith that he would ever be with you while he was here on earth, and he ultimately died of a broken heart. He has been with you, and watching," she said and then added, "How did he die?"

"He died of complications from heart surgery," I said. "So are you saying that he had a choice to stay or to leave the earth while he was on the operating table?"

"You need to understand that when we are facing a choice between life and death, there are many instances when we can make the decision to go either way. But there are always consequences," April explained. "In this case with Jay, his consequences were that you didn't get to live the life you were meant to have together, and obviously, neither did he. In the end, he thought he lost you, and decided to let go and return to spirit."

"This is a lot to take in." I didn't know what to do with this information, so I asked, "So where does this leave us?"

"The God or soul in Jay wants to ask the soul in your husband if he can take his place and be with you," she continued.

"Can that happen?" I asked. I was skeptical.

"Apparently," April said.

"How can that be? And what about my husband, Tom? Does he have a say in this?" I asked. "What happens to him?" I was in a miserable marriage, but he was still my husband, and I cared about him.

April continued. "Jay seems to know somehow that your husband, Tom, is unhappy here as well, and feels if he asked permission to change places with him, he would accept." She paused. "So in this case, Tom would go home to the spirit side."

"Really?" I asked. This was craziness. I knew Tommie was miserable, but this was too much. Too much to hope for, if I were honest with myself. Knowing how controlling Tom was, it didn't seem plausible. On so many levels, it made no sense. My head started to hurt.

"I have to say I don't know if I would have believed it either, but about a year ago, I was doing a reading for a man who sat down in front of me and asked, 'Do you know who I am?' I think he was testing me. I told him that I didn't think we had met before, and he announced, 'I'm a walk-in.' He was so cocky and obnoxious, and I can tend to be authority oppositional, so I said to him, 'Well then, you walked in backward, because you're talking out of your ass.'"

I laughed. April could be funny, and I loved how she got directly to the point. My kind of woman.

"Anyway, what I am trying to say is that there is such a thing as a walk-in. I have come across it before, although not very often, I have to admit," April stated. "What I'm also getting from the spirit side is that things can't end up the way they are supposed to unless you stop messing with your own head. In other words, Jay can't walk this earth with you until you stop doing this."

"Doing what?" I asked.

"Your mind's not in a good place," April continued. "You've bought into the system of the unconscious rules you were raised in. You became a human doing, not a human being. You must make a change in yourself, as I said. You need a good 'screw it' attitude. You can't get to where you want to be with Jay by staying on the same course. You worry about what other people think about you, and you need to stop that and get rid of your codependency."

"Codependency? Oh, boy, I guess you are right. I think I've always known it," I said sadly.

"Jay remembers you and who you were when you were younger, ready to take on the world. He loved your spunk, your can-do attitude. Your codependency is coming from you being in the box that you were raised to be in. Tom was raised to be in the same box. You did what was expected of you, whether it felt true or not. But when Jay knew you here, he encouraged you to be your real self. You had chutzpah. You were always happy, full of yourself. You went out and greeted the world!" April said while making a sweeping motion with her arm. "You had more of a sense of who you are. We need to bring you back to being the real you again so you can move forward with Jay."

"This is incredible. That is exactly who I used to be. I seem to have lost that person to cope with my life as it is. My life is not what I hoped for or what I expected. I worked so hard to create the life I wanted, but it didn't happen," I said, deep in thought.

"You started to become the expectation of who you thought you should be, not the person you are. Women do this all the time," April said. She looked at me. "We get comfortable in our boxes. The universe wants you to become awake and aware of yourself in the bigger scheme of things. You need to become aware of your life and no longer a victim of it."

"I'd love to," I said. "I will work on that, and myself." I was happy about this new mission for me. I was ready for a change. It was exhausting not being myself, acting like someone else to fit in.

"I swear this is one of the most unusual readings I've ever had," April said, laughing.

"Really?" I guessed I was not the only one who thought this conversation was a little out there—okay, maybe a lot out there. But I had to admit the thought appealed to me. Perhaps there really was something special going on here after all.

"Yes, I mean it. Let's continue, pull some cards, and see what else comes up," April said. I chose cards, and she began to assemble them in an intricate pattern I had never seen before.

She continued. "It talks about your inner growth and the strength in spirituality. There is safety around a move. Once you hold on to something, it's hard to let go. It's one of your greatest strengths. It's also one of your greatest weaknesses."

"It sounds a lot like stubbornness," I said, smiling.

"It also says you have far more options and choices than you give yourself credit for. You need to realize that life is a journey, not a destination. You need to let go and let God instead of trying to control the outcome of everything," she said.

I smiled at her. She had me pegged.

"Okay, let's look at this year. This says that the man of your past comes out of your past and goes into your future." April continued reading the tarot cards she placed in front of her on the table.

"It says that again?" I asked. "Well, it is definitely Jay—he is the one, and he passed away years ago," I repeated. "And my husband's name is Tom." I realized she already knew this, but I had no idea what else to say. This was a lot to take in. I was stumbling for words, hesitant yet hopeful.

"Yes, it does," April said.

"I guess I better listen," I said, laughing. The whole thing seemed unbelievable, but I wasn't going to simply dismiss it. Maybe it was true. Why not? Stranger things have happened.

"All you need to do is hear his voice to know it's him," April said. "His voice is melodic and deep. The bottom line here is to trust *your* inner voice, trust the guidance that you get. Remember that—if you trust your inner guidance, all you will need to do is hear his voice, and you will know it's him."

"Know it's Jay? So I just need to hear his voice to know that the soul has been transferred?" I asked, thinking that it all seemed too easy.

"I don't know all the details—all I know is that you've got some situations coming up. There seems to be some kind of a negotiation process around this. Between Jay and your husband, Tom."

"Negotiations?" I asked.

"Yes. This situation will change things, the outcome of things originally planned for your lives. Tom has things here on earth that he wanted to accomplish, things he wanted to do and to learn. Now all that will change. Jay and Tom will need to negotiate how the rest of your lives play out here in relation to how it was all originally planned on the other side," April explained.

"Our lives are planned? How does that work?" I asked.

"You plan your life before you come here—what you want to learn, what you want to create while you're here, to evolve as a soul," April replied.

Before I could ask more about this, she continued. "One of your guides just came in, talking to me. It's a he, not a she. He's saying, 'We want to make it clear to you that it is not just your act, that everybody is participating.' He's also saying that you are starting with a guilt trip, and he wants you to stop thinking that you somehow caused this to happen because of your unhappiness. Many are interested in the outcome and are participating in this. It is becoming much bigger than just the two of you."

"Others are interested in the outcome? Who else is participating? What is that all about?" I asked.

"I don't know at this point. They just want you to know that this is bigger than just the two of you and the process of this particular walk-in transfer is being watched very carefully. Almost like you are in a petri dish, under a microscope."

"Oh, my," I said, a little unnerved. I was not sure I was comfortable being under observation from the other side to this extent. But I was sure there was a reason for it, and there was nothing I could do about it, so I would wait and see how it all played out.

"Also, your own spiritual awakening will begin. It seems that you need to become more awake and aware as to who you are as a soul, a spirit, so the rest of this can happen. Almost like putting yourself in the right frame of mind," she continued.

"Oh, I guess that makes sense." It seemed like a huge undertaking, and I had no idea where to begin.

"This must seem overwhelming to you, a lot to take in," April said, right on cue.

"I do admit I am having trouble wrapping my head around it," I replied, chuckling.

"I have to admit that as well. This is not an average reading for me either," April said. "I'm intrigued by the whole thing. But I am just giving it to you as I see and hear the messages."

"Yes, I appreciate that," I replied.

She continued to look off into the distance, eyes searching. "Jay has a great voice. He's very self-aware, and he's being quite serious—not aggressive, just factual. It seems like he has nothing to prove. I'm impressed with him."

April looked back at the cards and continued. "There are things hidden at this point. But you will not be with the man you are with right now—you will be with the man you were meant to be with. So just be aware—you were not meant to be with the man you are with," April repeated, trying to make her point so it would stick. "There is a spiritual journey around this. I see you and the man of your heart walking off into the sunset together."

"Ohhh..." I said. "That's wonderful." My heart was filled with joy and longing, but I was having a very hard time putting it all into perspective.

"Strange but true," April said and looked at me, smiling. "I swear I don't make this shit up! The truth is stranger than fiction."

I laughed and said, "I bet you don't! Who could think up this story?"

The little timer went off, signaling we had five minutes left of our thirty-minute reading. "Is there anything else you want to know right at this point? Questions?" April asked.

"No," I said, smiling. "This was enough for one day, I think."

"Okay, well, it was great talking with you. I'm fascinated with what's happening with you," she said as she replaced the cards in the small velvet-lined box on the table.

"When will you be back to Rhode Island?" I knew I was going to want to hear more about this.

"September," she replied, smiling.

As we walked out of the room, April said to Glo, the owner of the bookshop, "That was definitely one of the strangest readings I have ever had." She turned to me and gave me a hug and said, "This should be quite a journey for you."

I hugged her back and thanked her. I was completely elated and confused at the same time.

"Thank you, April," I said. I was so happy to meet this woman who introduced me to this incredible journey.

"You're welcome," she said.

As I gathered my things to leave the shop, I paused as I saw April sit down at the table in the small hospitality room outside the reading room. Her appointment was late, so she decided to grab something to eat while she had the chance.

"How's it going? Glad to see you are finally getting a break," Glo said to April.

"It's going well. I seem to be doing okay with time, until now," April replied. "I have to say it again—that had to have been the strangest reading I've ever had."

"Why is that?" Glo asked.

"Well, from the minute she sat down, there was a man waiting for her from the other side," April explained.

"Happens all the time," Glo interjected.

"Yes, but this was different. His communication was so strong. The minute she sat down, he was standing behind where she was sitting, plain as day. The first thing he said to me was that he was the love of her life and she was the love of his life. But he died," April continued. "And I had this overwhelming feeling of love. I mean, I was really overwhelmed. And through the reading, I had such a sense of peace with it all. I knew it was real."

"Beautiful love story. Too bad he died," Glo said.

"But that is what is so extraordinary about this. He wanted to ask her permission to come back. To come back to earth as a walk-in," April said. "As we sat down and got started, I heard myself ask her, 'Do you know what a walk-in is?' That is not something I have ever asked anyone at a reading, in all my years of doing readings. I was really surprised."

"I've heard of walk-ins before, but I've never come across a real case of it. How did you make sense of it?" Glo asked.

"I'll tell you, I don't know if I would have believed it myself. But in the past few years, I have come across two cases of walk-ins. One was a man I met here for a reading, who just blurted out, 'I'm a walk-in.' I was very skeptical but continued with the reading, and it all seemed to make sense from what I was hearing."

Glo smiled at her.

"Then there was a woman who came in for a reading, and I told her I saw her son on the other side. She got upset and said, 'I have two sons that died!' I could see the one son in spirit, so I asked him where his brother was. He said he had already reincarnated as a three-year-old child. The mother said to me, 'Impossible. He only died a year ago!' I asked the brother if he could explain. All the facts could be verified between the brother on the other side and the mother in the reading. So at that point I realized it must be true that he was a walk-in. All the pieces fit. It has been so interesting to me to learn about this."

April got up for her next reading, who had finally arrived. "If this man trying to come back for Carolyn can pull it off, what an incredible love story!"

I finished collecting my things, and as I walked out of the shop, I felt as if I were on a cloud.

Thinking about the exchange I had just heard and what I had been told in the reading, I couldn't help wondering if this could this really be true? Could this really be happening? I couldn't wait to get back home to start researching what all this walk-in business was about. I didn't understand it at all, but I certainly was going to find out.

Over the next few months, I studied the phenomenon and scoured and devoured anything I could find on the subject, searching online, in libraries, and in bookstores. As I researched, it became evident that there was very little on the subject to be discovered. I found a few stories, video clips, and related articles, and I discovered that the jury was still out on the walk-in phenomenon as a whole. Some people understood what a walk-in was, while others thought it was simply hogwash and were not likely to believe it. It didn't matter to me what others thought about it. People could be closed minded, after all. It was my story, and I was excited to find out where it would lead me.

32

CAN'T HEAR YOU!

"Tom?"

No answer.

"Tommie?" I said a little louder. He either was ignoring me or couldn't hear me. Probably a little bit of both. I walked over to his favorite chair, where he was reading a magazine, and put my hand on his arm gently to get his attention.

"What!" he said, startled, with a sudden jerk, retreating from my touch. "What do you want?" he said with impatience.

"I just wanted to talk with you," I said, hurt and mad at the same time. There was no pleasing this man.

"Well, I can't hear you out of my left ear. You know that," he said. I thought it was more of a way of playing with me to put me off balance. Yet another way to be mad at me. He had a million reasons.

"Yes, I know. I thought you could hear me," I said. He never seemed to have this much trouble hearing anyone else. "I was thinking that it might be nice if we had some friends over for your birthday. It is a long weekend, and we could have a barbecue."

"Carolyn, I don't want to celebrate my birthday with anyone. I don't like parties, and you know I hate surprises." It amazed me how very different we were.

"But I thought maybe just a few people," I said. "It would be fun!"

"No, thanks," he said. "I don't want any fun." This was one thing that was true about him.

33

UNEXPECTED CHANGES

It was about three months later, and I couldn't wait to get back in to see April. I made an appointment for a Saturday afternoon. After doing some research and finding everything I could on-line about walk-in's, I wanted to see whether this was still true—or whether I had just made up the whole thing in my mind. I listened to the tape recording of that first reading many times, trying to get every detail, every scrap of information, and trying to decipher it.

April began. "Nice deep breath. You have two grandmothers wanting to say hi to you," she said. "Something has you in a tizzy— you're wondering which way to go."

She had that right—my mind was scattered, trying to figure out what to do with my life. I seemed to be in a race with myself to get somewhere. Unfortunately, I didn't know where that somewhere was.

She continued. "Fate. Your cards say that things will come back to you from the past. That circumstances will cause you difficulty for a while. And this says there will be a lot of unexpected changes. Everything in your life is a two-edged sword—there is a good side and a bad side of everything."

April stopped for a minute to communicate with spirit. "You are going to look at the past from a different perspective. It's almost like evaluating everything that has ever happened to you in your lifetime and refocusing where you want to go with it."

"Quite a task," I thought to myself. "Bring it on!"

"Things get delayed. Caution. Don't get frustrated if things don't go as fast as you want them to," she continued. "Big things are happening, and life is not without its struggles, but you have nothing to worry about."

"Well, that's good," I said softly. I was eagerly awaiting something about the walk-in situation we had spoken about at our last reading. Maybe she couldn't remember. She saw so many people, had so many life stories flow through her when she communicated with spirit. How could she possibly keep it all straight?

"I'm hearing that you need a vacation. You have a very creative nature. Your psychic energy is blowing sky high. The thing to be careful of is that you may want to spend more time in that world but you still have to live in this world."

"What do you mean when you say 'that world'?" I asked.

"When you open yourself up to your spirituality and become more awake and aware to the greater universe, it's easy to stay focused on that part of your life. It's a wonderful, comforting thing to do, filled with inspiration and peacefulness. The thing is that you have to be practical. You are still living in this world, and it can be harsh sometimes. Everyone will not be on the same page as you are." She paused. "You will have messages coming at you like that!" she said as she snapped her fingers.

"Will I be able to decipher those messages?" I asked. I very much wanted to be able to communicate with the afterlife like April, but I didn't know where to begin, how to do it. I realized she had a special talent, a gift, really. But that didn't mean I didn't as well, if I could just put my finger on it, open myself up to it. I knew it was in me somewhere.

"Yes, your intuition is right on. Your first thought, your first impression is always going to be the right one. And your intuition will never, ever lie to you. I believe it is our God voice talking," she continued. "Our intuition is similar to sending out magnetic fields. It hits other people and comes back to us with information. Kind of like pinging. It's whether or not we listen to our intuition that makes all the difference." She paused. "What would you like to focus on?" she asked.

Here was my chance to bring it up. I didn't want to interrupt April while she was on a roll—I just wanted to listen to see what came forth. But I was excited to find out more about Jay. "The last reading I had with you, there was something about a man from my past who died, and wanted to come back and possibly change places with my husband's body, as a walk-in. I've been studying that. I've listened to that recording of my last reading with you about a million times, and I'm so fascinated with it. Is that still true?"

April looked off into the distance, searching for something. After a moment she said, "Mm-hmm, it is. Yes, in fact I would say he is preparing for it right at this point."

"Good, so I wasn't misunderstanding what you said at our last reading," I said, happy this was still true. "I remember that he was right there, waiting to come through at my first reading with you. Most of the reading was about him," I explained.

"From what I understand from your guides and what I have heard in the past, there is usually a near-death experience with a walk-in." April paused. "And they are also telling me that the tenor of his voice will change."

"Okay, and you told me before that I would be able to tell the soul has been transferred from the tenor of his voice," I offered.

"Well, that's what they just said," she replied. "I'm getting that you would recognize his voice."

"Which would make sense, considering how special his voice was," I added. "I really loved that about him."

"I keep calling out to him, and all I keep getting is that he is getting ready. So there must be some prep he needs to complete in order to do what he wants to do as a walk-in," April said. "Also, you need to know that he can't do this unless your husband agrees to it."

"And he's not agreeing consciously, I'm assuming," I asked.

"No, it's that the God in him and the God in your husband have to come to an agreement," she explained. "There needs to be a contract between them to do this, soul to soul, on the spirit side."

"They have contracts on the other side?" I asked. I was intrigued.

"Yes. Everyone does. Before you come into this world, you write your contract: how long you stay, the lessons you expect to learn. You choose your parents," April said. "I think we may have talked about this a bit before."

"Yes, and I have been intrigued by the notion since then," I said. "That bit of information seems so amazing to me. We choose what will happen in our lives? We have a say in things?"

"We do. But we also have free will, which is often how we go off the rails," she said, smiling. "In this instance, Jay altered his contract with you because he gave up, lost hope when he died. When people lose hope, oftentimes they don't realize that there are more options than the one in front of them."

"Yes, I agree. It's sad. There is always another path to take if you look for it," I said. "And most people don't realize the effect their lives have on those around them, who are connected to them."

"Right," April continued. "Once you get to the other side, you see those threads of connections and what happened because we altered the contract. We also need to realize that Jay did alter your contract, and his as well. Seeing the results of that on the other side, seeing your unhappiness, drove him to want to seek a solution. The solution he came up with was to come back."

"This is all so amazing. It's also very hard to believe, I have to say," I said truthfully. I really didn't know what to make of all this.

"I'm sure it seems that way to you," April continued. "I must admit all this would be a very bizarre thing for me to say at a reading. It would not be on the top of my list. And honestly, it seems pretty special."

We both laughed at how ridiculous the whole thing sounded. Nonetheless, we both knew it was true and that we were on the inside track to something incredible.

April went back into her communicating trance. "I'm hearing that there will be some struggles, but not to worry; you will be with the man of your heart. There are options and choices; success is on hold, but it's being created. I think somehow instinctually, you are just going to know when this happens."

She became silent for a few moments, eyes searching. "I'm being told to tell you to watch and see but not to worry. There will be period of adjustment that will take place. Watch your dreams. A lot of information is going to come through your dreams, so keep a pen and paper next to your bed, and when you wake up from a dream about someone who has passed over, write down everything and anything as random thoughts. Don't think; just write. The trick is to not read the notes until after you have finished. When the pen stops, then you can read it. Let it flow before you read. Don't let your earth mind take over and fill in the blanks." She paused. "I believe they are trying to tell you some things through your dreams."

"Okay, I can do that." A pad and pencil were something I always had next to my bed at night. I often woke up with ideas, inspirations, and dreams I wanted to write down and think about later. I would love to get information about this.

"We are in a time now when we are going through a stage where we are fulfilling a prophecy. Part of that prophecy is that we are starting a new age. A new age has happened many, many times in the past. The reason I say that is that if you look at our history, there was a time when everyone thought the world was flat. Then there was a point when more people believed it was round than flat, and the tipping point happened. Well, now we are reaching that critical mass again."

"We as a whole?" I asked, thinking about Darwin's hundredth-monkey theory and what it took to reach critical mass, which, interestingly, was not much.

"Yes," she replied. "Oh, this is overwhelming. I have a man here in spirit that just came to me and said, 'Tell her I love her. I love her. I can't wait to hold her.'" April rubbed her arms as she looked at me, obviously overwhelmed with feeling the emotion.

"That's Jay," I said to April, beaming.

"Okay, all I know is that it is so overwhelming to me," she said, looking straight into my eyes. She continued, "There is a need for you to know to keep yourself free for opportunities. It shows things you are going to look at out of state. I'm getting that opportunities will come through the man of your heart. He has lots of determination. Ultimately, it says don't look backward. The woulda, coulda, shouldas aren't going to change what is."

"Okay," I said, thinking it would be quite a task for me to keep looking toward the future, not the past. But I could do it.

"There are things you will need to deal with from a practical standpoint, and don't be foolish," she said.

"What do you mean?" I asked.

"Your mind may be going through a fantasy of who he was and what your relationship was. Now you are a married woman with children. You have responsibilities. He's walking into these responsibilities, which are new to him. He didn't have children when he was here. You two weren't married or living together day to day. He is going to have a different way of looking at it all. Because the two of you have changed, you will move forward together in a new way. You have to be open to the changes, realize you are not still that twenty-two-year-old girl," she explained.

"No, I'm not. That's for sure," I said, smiling but trying to make sense of what I was hearing.

April continued. "What I am getting is that there is a part of you that is going to think that you are wishing this on your husband, that you want him to leave. You need to know that this can't happen if your husband doesn't agree to it. It is not wishful thinking on your part. Know that. Jay came through to you to ask your permission to come back to you, to make sure you felt the same way he did. After you said yes, he was then free to ask Tom if he wanted to trade places. Tom agreed without hesitation. He is unhappy here. He wants to leave. Just remember it is nothing you have done other than be loved by a man so much he wants to come back to you from the spirit side."

April paused and looked at me seriously. "Do you understand?"

"I...I do," I said, overwhelmed. This was big stuff we were talking about. I knew I was out of my league and needed to follow my heart and instincts. "That's good to hear—that's exactly where I was going with this," I replied, somewhat relieved because I *had* wondered whether I had somehow willed Tom to leave.

"I have one of your guides here. It's a man, not a woman." April laughed and continued. "He's saying to me that he wants you to know that it's not wishful thinking, and he's shaking his finger at me to make his point," she said to me as she wagged the index finger of her left hand to demonstrate. "And it's his left hand. He's very adamant. It is not wishful thinking on your part. You did not cause this to happen."

I must admit I was a bit relieved.

April went on. "So ultimately, one of the first rules—and this is universal—is that no one is allowed to interfere with your free will."

"Of course, we all have free will," I agreed. "But if everything is figured out ahead of time, if you plan your life, choose your lessons and your parents before you are reincarnated, why bother if it can all change?"

"The truth is with free will, you get to make up the rules as you go, your decisions on how those lessons will come about. It isn't completely planned beforehand. In all instances, we are making it up as we go, with guidance from the other side," April explained.

"It's sad that so many people are living unconsciously, on autopilot. They need to realize it's their lives and they have control to make them good or not," I added.

"However, you and Jay had an agreement from the other side, as we said, to part ways and then get back together. When he died, it took those original plans off the table. What should have happened in the second half of your life never did. Remember he said he died of a broken heart," April said, "because you were supposed to be together. If he hadn't died, you would have lived the authentic life you were supposed to. You would have left Tom and married Jay down the road."

"How can that be?" I asked April. "He died, so that was not our path." I wasn't sure that our lives were destined to be lived a certain way. I knew we had free will, and I wanted to understand this.

"Even though his soul knew you were to be together, he didn't believe it on a conscious level," April continued.

"You mean when he was going through his surgery, he could have chosen to live?" I asked.

"Yes, most likely," April went on. "But he thought he lost you forever. He was very sad and had tears welling up in his eyes when he came through to tell me about this the first time. It was pretty intense. He gave up when he was here. He simply thought he lost you forever."

I began, "I remember after I found out that Jay died, Tom started to sound like him. Making the same adorable noises with his mouth and making gestures that were just like Jay as well. It was so evident to me that it was Jay getting a message to me. I just didn't know what it was."

"That's called stepping in," April explained. "That was just Jay's way of connecting with you. I believe he has been around you since he died. Watching over you."

"Which would explain how he knew I was so unhappy," I said, thinking out loud. "But how in the world did he know to ask Tom if he wanted to leave earth and return to heaven?" This all still seemed to be a bit much, but I was opening up more and more to the possibility. It felt good to open my mind to the possibilities.

"If he was watching you, he was watching Tom as well and must have seen he was unhappy too. Maybe he thought Tom would consider this if approached and given the option," she replied. "Do you see how this could happen?"

"Yes, I guess so," I said. "But still…"

"I'm hearing that with a little determination on Jay's part, things are going to turn out better than you think. I'm getting that there will be victory with the man of your heart. Also, a lot of people are going to put their two cents into your business. You need to trust your own instincts, trust yourself. Don't be naïve," she continued.

"Do we have any idea how long this is going to take?" I asked. If this was going to happen, I wanted to get on with it.

"You know, it's like Jay doesn't have control over when things are going to happen with Tom and this transfer. But he did just come in and said, 'June, June, tell her June!'" she said, pretending to be Jay, whispering loudly. "There is something about an eighteen-month waiting period. It seems that during this period of time, either of them can change his mind about the transfer. So it's understandable that Jay wants to make sure he waits the eighteen months to begin the process so Tom can't back out."

"Yes, that would be a disaster, I'm sure," I said while counting the months in my head. Finally, I had something concrete to work with. "But I wonder why eighteen months."

"It's like this," April began. "When you are born, your soul has eighteen months to decide to complete this life. It is the same in this situation for a walk-in."

"Oh, that's so interesting," I replied.

"But do remember that Jay does not have full control over everything, but I guess it's the marked time at this point. And you will see a distinct difference in the way your husband acts and looks. He will become withdrawn. He may seem like he's giving up. He may just have a heart failure and the other soul takes over. Or it could be something that happens in his sleep. It doesn't have to be a major accident. In any case, whatever happens will follow the universal laws. It is not esoteric. We have an intelligent universe, not a random universe," April said.

"April, does it seem to you that Tom is like a pawn in all this? Like someone is just taking over his life?" I asked. "It's kind of scary, when you think about it..."

"He's not a pawn. He has eighteen months to be with you, to reconsider if he wants to leave. He has full control over his negotiations," she replied. "He can agree or disagree. It's his choice."

"So I guess he's made his choice," I said. It hurt a little bit that this was the choice he had made.

"Also, I'm being told you will withdraw emotionally for a time to deal with all this. In other words, you don't have to walk away from someone to divorce yourself from him. You will go through a grieving process. You are married to the man and, on some level, love him," April explained.

"Yes, I do love him. Just a different kind of love," I said, deep in thought. "Okay."

April giggled as she said, "Jay said he would remember me. He is telling me how much he is looking forward to meeting me." She smiled. "He's saying to me, 'I'm going to remember you. And I can't wait to meet you. They gave me permission to remember you,'" April reported.

"That's awesome," I said. Jay and April were becoming fast friends, even in these extraordinary circumstances.

"I hear from the other side that there are unexpected changes coming. You have an opportunity to be happy. I know it seems illogical, but on some level spiritually, it is all true. Everything that is going to happen, everything that we are talking about here, there is a logic to it. Trust it. Watch the little girl—the inner child in you. It's where the insecurities are, and our own insecurities can sabotage ourselves and what we truly want in our hearts," April said. "Stay in this world, and stay focused on where you're going."

"I will trust it. I do already. I just want to find out all I can about it," I replied.

"So try to keep yourself grounded, stay the course, and let it all unfold," April said.

"Easier said than done, but I'll do my best. Grounded, huh? Okay. Maybe some rocks in my pocket?" I said, laughing.

"That will work," April said, smiling at me. "Crystals and spiritual rocks can help with your own spiritual awakening as well as help you deal with what's happening. I know it is all wonderful and a beautiful love story, but it has to be doing quite a job on you! It could help you with your part of the process."

"Thanks, April. I'll give it a try. And yes, it is a lot to take in and process," I said, smiling. "But I'm happy to have it to work through."

"I'm getting that in the future, you could end up doing what I'm doing. You will go after opportunity. You are going to end up in your own business. You will be supporting groups of people that do what I do," April continued.

"Really?" I exclaimed. "I'd love that!"

"It is what I'm getting. This is the business of psychics, spirituality. So this is working with, working around, or doing something connected to that. Something to do with the New York–Connecticut area. It almost looks like you could be a mentor for people. It's almost like an agent of sorts for people who have these abilities."

"Yes, I could totally see myself doing something like that!" I said. "I would love to put my business mind to use in that regard. To somehow have a hand in expanding consciousness with others."

"So look into that. See what it takes to do it. It's no different from being a talent agent—marketing, negotiating, contracts, and so on. The business side of things." April went on. "There are people who are really talented. For instance, I have a business up north, and my husband used to take care of the financial side, as well as the business side, and I took care of the talent side. Ultimately, I don't want to do both. It becomes very difficult to work when all you want to do is be the talent. So in order for us to be successful, we need someone to take care of the administrative and business side of things. So in essence it would be a win-win situation. I'm going to say you need to do some research and look into it."

"Happily," I said.

"A lot of things are up in the air. You will be spiritually creating over the next two years," she said. "Also, I do believe Jay will know he is a walk-in when he gets here."

"Wonderful!" I said excitedly. It was almost too much to hope for.

"That's rare," April said seriously as she looked at me.

"That's very interesting," I said, while I was actually thinking it was really cool.

April smiled widely, and with a twinkle in her eye, she said, "Jay is here. He just had an 'oh, shit' moment. He realized that when he comes back, he is going to have to support you and the boys. He is very serious about this. He is going to have to figure it out. He wants to support you in the way you deserve to be supported."

I was dumbfounded. I hadn't even thought about that or put two and two together. Of course, Tom and Jay were worlds apart in personality, knowledge, talents, and, in this case specifically, their careers.

"This bodes the question, how much is he going to be able remember of his past life, since he has to take on Tom's knowledge to take care of you?" April pondered.

That was sad to think about. I didn't want Jay to have to give up anything he loved to do or to be less than happy to take care of us and continue in Tom's job. I would do all that I could as well to make it easier for him. I knew we would figure it all out. I had complete faith in us.

34

PARTRIDGE IN A PEAR TREE

I was driving in the car, listening to the local all-holiday station on the radio. It was about three weeks before Christmas, and I was heading to a reading with April in the spiritual bookstore where she scheduled readings for her clients in Rhode Island and nearby Massachusetts.

By this point, she stayed at my home with my family when she was in Rhode Island, and we often stayed up until the wee hours of the morning discussing spirituality, organized religion, the history of religion, what it was like on the other side, and how it all worked. I asked question after question and taped all our conversations so I could listen and decipher later. I couldn't seem to satisfy my curiosity. I looked forward to the time we spent together. She had been a professional medium for over forty years, and had seen—and heard—a lot.

As I stopped at a red light, I checked my wallet to make sure I had some cash to pay for the reading. Whenever April was offering readings in Rhode Island, I liked to support her, since it was her livelihood. She was as interested in the walk-in topic as I was, and just as fascinated with the process we were privy to.

Once when I tried to pay her for one of our tutoring sessions, which consisted of me asking a million questions and her explaining and teaching me, she refused. I asked why, and she explained she loved being involved in what was happening with me and that she was learning as much as I was. We agreed that I would pay for readings I officially scheduled from time to time, but we were on this journey together.

So when I booked an official appointment, I paid for the reading. We had long since passed the professional-client relationship and were now close friends, but I didn't want to take advantage of our friendship.

I began thinking about the upcoming holiday. I liked to be done and ready for Christmas Day ahead of time and did my shopping mostly online—from small purveyors whenever possible. The holiday crowds were not for me, and the commercialism of the holiday aggravated me to no end. So we tried to keep it low key and had a nice, quiet family holiday celebration. Christmas was not a spend-fest at our house; it was just a time to be together and enjoy one another's company.

As I pulled into the parking lot and was looking for a space to park, "The Twelve Days of Christmas" came on the radio. I was a few minutes early, so I decided to stay in the car and sing along with the radio. This was one of my favorite holiday songs—I loved to try to keep up with the words when it started backward from the twelfth day, twelve drummers drumming, to the first day, a partridge in a pear tree. I did pretty well this time. I usually mixed up the maids a-milking with the pipers piping, but today I missed only a beat or two. I laughed and thought to myself, "I'm such a cornball."

I finished my little concert in the car and walked into the book-store. I was greeted by Glo asking whether I would care for anything to drink. I refused and sat down to wait my turn.

Just a minute or two later, April came out of the small room in the back where she did her readings. She said good-bye to the person with whom she had the reading, and turned to me and said, "Ready?"

"Yep," I said, getting up gingerly and following her into the room, and she closed the door. The decorating and the little back room seemed so bohemian to me, but the ambiance seemed to work.

"Oh, those are pretty!" I said to her, pointing to the new deck of cards she was shuffling. "New deck?" I asked.

"Yes, aren't they? I love the colors. It's funny—I've been asked a couple of times today if they were going to work because they were new. People don't understand it really has nothing to do with the cards themselves. It's so much more than that," April said.

She placed her hands on my left hand and asked me to say my first name. Her hands were warm.

"Carolyn," I said.

She started communication right away. "You've got two people here, your grandmother and a woman who appears to be an aunt on your mother's side..."

As I thought about who this woman that was coming through to communicate was, April giggled. I looked at her, smiling, wondering what was going on. She laughed a little bit more and said, "He's singing to me. It's Jay. He's got a good voice," she continued. "Not a great voice, but a good voice," she said, laughing as if it were an inside joke.

"That's so funny! I said the same thing when we were together when he was here. I accused him of not being a real singer, and he pretended he was offended by that. We joked about it often," I exclaimed.

April demonstrated. "'My true love gave to me...' You know, that 'partridge in a pear tree' song. What's the name of that?"

I felt a shiver come over me. "This is amazing!" I said to April with a huge smile on my face. "I was just singing that song in the car—trying to keep up with it. I was having a grand ole time entertaining myself."

"Well, he heard you and wants you to know he's with you," April said, smiling.

"That's so nice," I said. The thought of this warmed my heart. This whole process of the walk-in soul transference seemed to me to be taking forever. I was so unhappy at home with Tom; it was hard being in a loveless marriage, and to make matters worse, every time

I tried to be kind or reach out to him, be friends, have a laugh together, I was met with snide comments, attitude, and ignorance.

"That's sweet," I said, trying to get my point across. It was nice to think about.

"How is everything at home with Tom?" April asked, as if reading my mind. But then again, knowing April, she probably was.

"He's about the same. Miserable. Unhappy. Mad all the time, short fuse," I said. "I can't wait until Jay gets here." It sounded so trite to me to utter those words. As if I were waiting for a train to pull into the station or something and Jay would arrive and change my life instantly and forever.

"Well, it's not going to be as simple as Tom out, Jay in. There is a process to this. Jay is saying to me, 'It's complicated.' They are getting things ready. He says he must take classes before he returns here. And he is taking them now."

"What kind of classes?" I asked her. I wondered what kind of classes a spirit would take.

"Classes to prepare him for the transfer. There are things he has to learn about your life, Tom's life, how it will work once he is here," April was saying to me with that glazed look in her eyes. Whenever she was communicating with spirit, she had a faraway look in her eyes, as if she were somewhere else—which she usually was. We called it her "Elvis has left the building" look.

She began again. "I don't know what the classes entail. I just know they are necessary. He just told me, 'I don't need to go to the class on birthing, since I'm going into an adult body,'" April said. Shrugging her shoulders, she added, "You just can't make this shit up!"

I thought about this. "I wonder about these classes. How that works. I mean, is there a Walk-In 101 class?" I asked, giggling. "I wonder if it is like the movie *Nosso Lar*. Have you seen it?" I asked.

"I think we watched it together at some point, didn't we? But I don't remember it all," she replied.

"It is a movie filmed in Portugal, and I think it was the highest-grossing movie in the country or something. I loved it, and it put so much into perspective for me about the afterlife, reincarnation, what we go though, how it all works…fascinating. Anyway, I wonder…" I said thoughtfully.

"It seems that there are contracts that need to be drawn up between the two of them. Jay just said to me, 'It's something about the stars or planets aligning or some other nonsense.'" She laughed. "He's funny," she said.

Sometimes I had trouble understanding it all from my limited earthbound perspective. I was a planner and a black-and-white thinker, so sometimes that made it even harder. Fortunately, I had an open mind and complete faith in the spirit side.

"Jay wants to make sure they wait that eighteen months so after the switch is made, Tom can't change his mind. This is a big thing for Jay. He wants everything to go smoothly," April said and then stopped talking, deep in spiritual communication. She looked at me seriously and said, "Do you have any idea what this man is giving up for you? How much he loves you? He is giving up everything to be here with you."

"Yes," I said. "I'm really starting to understand the intensity of what all this means and what he must have had to go through to be with me." I had tears in my eyes. "I feel so blessed." It began to sink in, just what this wonderful man was doing to be with me and to share the rest of our lives together, to try again.

April looked at me and then went back into communication mode. "Carolyn, do you know how we assumed that Jay would just wake up and be Jay after the soul transfer?"

"Yes, I do," I said.

"Well, it seems there is more to it than that. Just a little hiccup," she said, smiling. "It's not going to be so easy."

"Uh-oh," I said, feeling a bit deflated.

"They are telling me that Jay does have permission to remember this. He will know what happened," April reported. "Your guides are telling me that he will become awake and aware to this at some point.

Most likely once the process of this transfer is complete, but it will take time."

"Oh, that is wonderful news! You mentioned that at our last reading as well. I was hoping he could remember!" I said to April. Even if it was not going to be as easy as I thought, at least he would remember everything. I wanted so much to have Jay back—in any form—and for him to remember all this opened some incredible possibilities for communication, partnership, and even deeper connection. "I just miss him so much," I said.

"He knows," April said. "He wants you to know that he's with you every day," she said. "No, actually he's saying that he's with you every minute of every day. He wants you to know that."

"Thank you for watching over me, Jay," I said as I looked upward. It felt perfectly natural, talking to the ether. I was moved by what was happening. All of it.

I looked back at April as I heard her say, "I'm so overwhelmed. Something is totally overwhelming me…" she began. "'I can't wait to see you, hold you, love you.'" April continued communicating Jay's words from spirit. "'I can't wait to be with you.'"

I brought my hand to my heart gently. "I feel exactly the same way," I said.

"Your grandmother on your father's side is here to say hello. She wants you to know she has been asked to be the one to communicate with you during this transition with your husband and the man of your heart. She is honored to be in this role," April explained. "Somehow, she is involved in the process that is coming and your new life."

April paused. "She wants you to understand that your path in this life was supposed to go a certain way, but your life went another way. She is saying, 'It was not supposed to be like this.' What was supposed to happen was that you would marry Tom, you would have your children, you and Tom would part ways, and you would get back together with Jay. But as you know, he died, and that didn't happen," April reported.

"Mm-hmm," I said. My mind was far away. "I understood that from our first reading." I guess the guides really wanted me to understand that point.

"These changes that are coming are not what you expected. But it has put you two on a new path, with new beginnings. She is saying something about seminars and you and Jay working together."

"That would be nice…" I said.

April began again. "There was something bigger you and Jay were supposed to do here on the earth plane, and when he died, it didn't happen. Your grandmother is saying she thinks that is another reason they have given Jay permission to do this, to be with you again."

"I wonder what that could be," I said.

"It seems that there is still some negotiating going on with this. But as you know, Tom has agreed to do this," April reported.

"Oh, thank heaven Tom agreed," I said, a little relieved. "They are negotiating? I wonder what about…"

"I'll see if I can find out more about it," April said.

"Thanks. The simple fact that they are negotiating is so interesting to me," I replied.

"Me too." Then, changing the subject, April continued. "Jay is saying that it's going to be funny to be called by a different name. He's also saying that he's not too thrilled with the body he is going to be in…" April continued, smiling. I joined her in a giggle. Tom had the body of a businessman who sat behind a desk all day. Jay had been an actor and singer and constantly on the go. They couldn't have led two more different lives here on earth.

"And there seems to be negotiations going on with this between Jay and Tom. One of the things that Tom wants is for Jay not to be able to have sex with you when he comes back," she continued.

"What?" I asked, annoyed. "This is something they are negotiating? Wouldn't I have a say in this? Why would Tom care? We haven't had sex in nine or ten years!" I said, exasperated. "He wants absolutely no part of me physically. If I reach out to touch him or even brush up against him by accident, he pulls away like I'm on fire."

"I guess Tom doesn't want to have sex with you, but he doesn't want anyone else to either!" April said. We both laughed, but I was not happy about it.

"That sounds about right," I said sarcastically.

April began again. "I'm being told that you two are going to get married again."

"Aww!" I exclaimed. "That is so romantic."

"You are going to renew your vows and get married again," April said, "and walk off into the sunset together. You will be with the man of your heart. This is an ultimate love story. Beyond time and space," April said matter-of-factly. "Such an incredible journey you two are on."

35

DROPS OF JUPITER

"**D**rops of Jupiter in her haaair!" I sang as I walked through the chilly night air.

I loved walking the dogs at night, up and down the quiet streets of our neighborhood. I was alone most of the time on my walks, and it was a great place to collect my thoughts, in the quiet of the night, under the moon and the stars.

As I walked, I pondered what all this meant—that Jay was coming back to be with me, that Tommie had agreed to leave and return to spirit. I was excited and grateful Jay loved me so much that he was willing to leave what I could only imagine was paradise to return to me on this earth.

On some level, I was also sorry that Tommie wanted to leave. I was sorry that I couldn't be the wife, partner, and friend that he needed. I was thinking how sad it was that Tom had given up so easily, that he was so unhappy here. I wondered what my part in this might have been. There are two sides to every story, and I was not perfect, by any stretch of the imagination. But that was water under the bridge, and everything was moving forward, even if it did seem as if it was taking forever.

The negotiating between the two souls was just about complete, and now it was time to wait. As I put the earphones on and listened to my iPod, as I did every night while walking, my theme song came on.

"Now that she's back in the atmosphere…with drops of Jupiter in her haaair…" I sang. "Reminds me that there's time to change—eh, eh, eh, eh, eh-hey," I sang. I couldn't wait for the change that was coming for me.

"Tell me! Did you sail across the sun? Did you make it to the Milky Way to see the lights all faded? And that heaven is overrated!" I continued singing with emotion. I didn't think heaven could be overrated, but to each his own. "Now that she's back from that soul vacation—tracing her way through the constellation, hey, hey…"

"Drops of Jupiter" by Train was what I considered my theme song for what was happening in my life at this point. I listened to it just about every night while I walked and thought about what was to come and what was leaving from my life. So much of that song made sense to me, or at least I created my own meaning for the lyrics to make it all fit. It was a comfort that someone, even if just a voice on my iPod, understood.

I bellowed out my favorite line in the song: "Told a story about a man who is too afraid to fly, so he never did land!" Singing was such a release for me. The best way I knew to release stress, although not so great for folks within earshot.

"And tell me, did Venus blow your mind? Was it everything you wanted to find? And did you miss me while you were looking for yourself out there?" I bellowed. "And did you finally get a chance to dance along the light of day? Na na na na, na na na na, na ahh-ahh-ahh…"

Unfortunately, I had a terrible singing voice. But it didn't matter; if the music was blaring, in my head I sounded like Carly Simon. No one seemed to notice, except a dog or two letting me know they were there.

As I walked and sang, I could picture Jay walking along the sun, smiling down at me, telling me, "I'll be there soon." I was thinking about Jay coming back and what our lives would be like. How would things change? How would they be the same? We were different people now. I knew it would all be okay, and at the very least as wonderful as it had been when we were together when we were younger.

That night I had a very vivid dream, which I think was probably a lot more than a dream. I was sleeping in the guest room. Tom didn't want to sleep with me; he said I snored and he couldn't sleep. The fact was we just didn't want to be close, and it seemed the path of least resistance.

As I lay there in the twin bed, just before waking, I had a strong sense that Jay was with me. I was in that delightful dream state when you are half-awake and half-asleep. It felt as if Jay was whispering to me and gently hugging me to reassure me that everything would be wonderful and he would be here soon. It was a beautiful answer to the questions I had the night before on my walk.

I fluffed up my pillows and tried to get back to sleep. This was one dream I wanted to continue.

36

MAKING A BIT OF HISTORY ON THE OTHER SIDE

April was connected to spirit as we got started with our reading. "I'm talking with Jay on the spirit side, and I see some men in oatmeal-colored robes off in the distance. They seem to be listening intently to our conversations. I am speaking with them now. They have been with us before. They seem very interested in the whole process that will be taking place. It seems that they have a vested interest in the outcome of this particular walk-in transfer. They are looking to see how it will all play out. It has further implications than just the two of you."

"Hmm," I interjected, completely fascinated. "This must be what my guide was saying to us last time we met for a reading. Something about this situation being bigger than just us—Jay and me. That more were participating. I wonder what that means." My curiosity was in overdrive.

April continued. "It seems that this has never been done before, in this way. In other words, where somebody approached another and requested to take over his body and continue his life. This could have larger consequences on the spirit side, helping them in some way."

"Really? This little story of ours could help the universe? That's pretty incredible to think about," I said, more than just a little dumbfounded. "Talk about giving back," I added, smiling.

"It sounds that way," April replied, eyes searching. She continued, "They are explaining how this transfer will take place. One guide will stand with Jay. One guide will stand with Tom. And a third guide will make the transfer of the silver cord between them. They said it will happen in a breath." April paused. "This is what they are aiming at, hopefully happening in his sleep."

"The silver cord that connects us all to our souls on the other side?" I asked.

"Yes," April continued after a short silence. "They seem to be concerned that Tom may balk or cause trouble during the transfer. So they are being very careful about it all."

"Balking at the transfer, even after he agreed and everything has been negotiated?" I asked. "What ramifications could that have? I wonder."

"They told me it could create trauma. There also seems to be a bit of an uproar on the other side about how much they should communicate with us, how many details we should have." April paused and then continued. "I'm getting that this is a big deal to the spirit world and this was unheard of before."

"That blows my mind," I said.

"It blows my mind too," April said. "Again, I'm hearing that this kind of transfer has never been done this way before. It seems like this is making history in the spirit world. And naturally, they don't want to cause trauma to either of them."

She paused. "They are carefully trying to figure out how this is all going to take place and what will happen afterward, the consequences of it all. Normally, someone from the physical world is begging to leave. 'I don't want to be here. I want to come home.' Many of them are suicidal, or they are on an operating table after an accident and just let go, decide to leave, even if they still have things here they want to do."

"Like they are just done with life here, had enough?" I questioned.

"Yes, and they are thinking, 'Let me go, please let me go.' And someone from the spirit side offers, 'I've got things I want to do and things I want to finish on the earth, so I'll take over and finish your life.' That's normal."

She paused, collecting her thoughts. I didn't think "normal" was the right word for something like that, but what did I know anyway?

"My guides in spirit want me to know that it was always a crisis needed to make the switch. It was always someone here on earth asking. Not someone from the spirit side asking. That was the big difference: Jay asked for this to happen from the spirit side."

April paused, her eyes still searching. I was awestruck.

"Then the higher echelon, the Council, started to pay attention and got involved. This was unheard of before. But they saw the possibilities," she reported.

"The possibilities? And what the hell is a council?" I asked. This all seemed too farfetched.

"It's a body of elders that makes sure everything stays together as a synchronistical world. They are God's council to make sure the laws of nature are followed and free will is not interfered with. There are many councils that make up the Grand Council. One of the councils seems to be interested in this."

"And it all started with this," I said, completely overwhelmed.

"And it all started with this, with Jay wanting to be with you," April replied.

"Wow, the pressure!" I said, laughing but feeling the importance of it all. "Oh, my gosh."

"Well, it became bigger than just the two of you, and I clearly had the impression from the other side that they were beside themselves—well, not exactly, but concerned. 'How much can we say to them? How much do we actually know about how this is all going to happen, to play out?'"

"Maybe they felt as though they needed to answer those questions for us," I said. "Or needed us to cooperate in some way, help from this side somehow."

"I think they are giving us the pieces along the way, and as time goes on, we will have been given enough pieces to put a lot of the puzzle together," April replied, deep in thought.

"This is incredible. I feel like we are privy to the inside scoop of something big..." I said. "This whole thing is so overwhelming to me. Why do we even know this? Why have they let us in on as much as they have?" I asked.

"Because they felt you needed to know, for whatever reason," April replied. "And part of it was my nosy self, asking so many questions on the spirit side, because I am so fascinated with it as well."

"Yeah," I said softly, deep in thought. "Makes sense, I guess."

"Do you see what I'm saying?" April asked me, laughing.

"I do, but I guess what I didn't understand was how far reaching it is," I said.

"But for you, it's a love story. It's a man who loved you so much that he went and found a way to walk back into this world so you could have the life you deserved," April said emotionally.

"And that's what's most important. The love," I said softly, overwhelmed with the feeling of gratitude for what Jay was doing to be together with me again.

"Yes," April said. "It's that simple."

37

EIGHTEEN MONTHS UP YET?

"Tommie is gray, withdrawn. Something is going on with him. He's almost despondent," I said to April. She and I were having a glass of wine in front of a roaring fire in the family room. It was nice. I loved these conversations. We could pick apart, analyze, and try to make sense of everything we had learned about this process and this spiritual journey we were on. So much had happened in the months since I met April. We talked often and had become close friends.

"Has it been eighteen months?" April asked. "Remember we were told that there was some type of eighteen-month waiting period before this could take place."

"Let's see. When did we first meet?" I asked aloud and started counting back in my mind. "We met in June, a year and a half ago. It is just about eighteen months now. Maybe it was a waiting period for the process to start, and to plan the actual transfer of the two souls. If that is how it's done on the other side." This was still confusing to me. Sometimes I felt I was just bumping around in the dark, trying to make sense of it all.

"That would make sense," April said. "Tom had eighteen months to change his mind, and Jay didn't want to ask for the transfer to be completed before that, in case he did."

"I thought it was eighteen months until the transfer actually happened, not just the go-ahead. But this makes sense," I said.

"It does," April replied.

"Have you always had this gift?" I asked April. She was in her early sixties and had been teaching spiritual classes and working with educators, businesses, and cold cases with law enforcement for years. I was wondering how it all began for her.

"I've had it my whole life. I remember when I was three talking to my guide, who was huge, and reminded me of an oak tree, and I thought I was talking to God. He would walk and talk with me all the time. Then my angel took over and has led me through the rest of my life to help me with my personal spiritual journey and my communication with the other side," she said.

"Well, you certainly have a special gift. I'm happy you are sharing it with me," I said, smiling at her.

She smiled back at me. "My pleasure. I'm enjoying it all so much. This is probably the most fascinating and incredible thing I've come across from the spirit side. I'm grateful to be a part of it."

38

IT HAPPENED LAST NIGHT

"Oh, man, there is so much laundry to do..." I said as I stuffed laundry from the floor of our bedroom into the makeshift laundry basket, which was really an oversized wastebasket. "I really need to get another one of these," I thought. Housework was not my thing. I hated doing it, but it had to get done. I had taken the day off from work to get caught up with some things at home.

Just as I finished bellyaching, my cell phone rang. I glanced at the phone, which was charging on my nightstand, and saw it was April. I reached for the phone. I knew April was in Arizona at a Tesla conference, so it must have been something important.

"I was wondering if anything had happened with Tommie yet," she said.

"No, not yet. But his mood, health, and attitude have gotten steadily worse," I replied. "I am waiting patiently but haven't noticed anything out of the ordinary with Tom. But he looks terrible physically. His skin has a gray pallor, and he's lethargic too. No interest in anything, grumpier than usual."

"Oh, interesting," she said. "Didn't your guide tell us that he would become despondent and falter in his health before the transfer took place?"

"Yes, I remember that. We had to watch his health..." I replied.

We were about a month past the marked time of June that Jay had told us the transfer was going to happen. I was thinking for some reason that the transfer would have happened on Jay's birthday, or at least the birthday he had when he was walking this earth. That date was June 23. It was now July 28.

"Okay, well. I had to call you right away because I just got a message from the spirit side. They told me that the transfer happened last night. 'It's done. Call her up, and tell her the switch is made,' they said to me and wanted me to relay the message to you. Have you noticed anything, maybe could tell that something was different with Tom?" April asked.

"Really?" I asked. "Last night?" I thought back to the night before. Nothing seemed different. "Wow, this is amazing..." I said. "It doesn't seem any different. But I will watch closely for any changes or hints of changes."

"Yes, watch him closely. They told me the transfer happened last night, during Tom's sleep. Also, Tom did balk at the last minute, just as they suspected he might. He thought it was a trick. They calmed him down though, and everything worked out," April said. "There was some trauma involved. They are concerned that it may affect Jay in that body. They said it is all okay for now."

"Thank heaven. I'm glad it is all okay. I was wondering what was going to happen there," I said. "Thanks for letting me know, and I will keep you posted."

"Okay," April said. "It will be interesting to see how this all plays out."

"Definitely. I can't wait to see what changes and when. We will be together this week too. We are taking Sam away to Hershey Park on Wednesday, so I will keep a close eye on him."

"Great, I'd love to hear all about it! Call me when you get back," April said.

"I will!" I responded. We hung up, and I hugged myself with an elation I hadn't felt in a long time. I was so happy; I felt so loved. It was a wonderful feeling. This was the beginning of something wonderful. Uncharted territory, but wonderful just the same.

That was it; our lives changed with a single phone call.

39

IT'S BEEN TEN YEARS!

It was a Sunday, the day after the transfer happened, and the family was home relaxing. It was pouring rain, and it was colder than usual. After the news from April earlier, I was watching my husband intently. I was looking for anything that would signify a change, something different about him. He had been happy most of the day but a little groggy. He had complained that there was a soreness through his chest and upper arms. Thinking back on how the actual process of the transfer would happen, I thought it made sense. I would think something like that couldn't be easy on a body.

It was tough. I was holding back the urge to ask him whether he felt different, but I knew I shouldn't push him. He needed to wake up to this realization on his own.

I had been instructed by our guides through readings to let him wake up slowly and at his own pace. Let it all come naturally to him. His unconscious mind was running the show now, and I knew it would take time to get him seated into his new surroundings and his new body. So I would wait. Maybe not too patiently, but I would wait.

Later that night, I was in the bathroom getting a few last-minute things packed for a trip we were taking to the amusement park in Hershey, Pennsylvania, with Sam and one of his young friends—something I was dreading to do with Tom. He hated amusement parks and crowds; the whole atmosphere made him roll his eyes and made him extremely grumpy. I wondered how this trip would be now that the transfer had happened.

Tommie/Jay was already in bed. I wondered what I should call him. I needed to come up with something. After a minute, I decided to refer to him as Jaymie, a combination of Jay and Tommie.

"Brrr," I said rubbing my arms with my hands to warm myself up. "It's freezing!"

Jaymie looked at me from the bed with a grin. "Come here. Let me warm you up." I noticed that his smile had a bit of the devilish grin Jay had when he talked about making love.

"Oh, boy..." I thought. "Is this really happening?" I went over to the bed and snuggled down into his open arms. We kissed.

It had been over ten years since I had made love, and here it was, back in my life and with the man I loved so dearly. Or at least some of him. It was sweet, and awkward; we were a little out of practice. Either way, it was wonderful. Afterward I felt the sweet peacefulness of a woman who was truly loved. So regarding the negotiations Tom and Jay had before the transfer regarding having sex, Jay, 1; Tom, 0.

The next morning, when I woke up, his arms were still around me. I wasn't dreaming. This was the beginning of my life back with the man of my heart. I looked up and quietly said thank you to my guides, the angels, and the universe.

40

ROLLER COASTERS AND CANDY BARS

I woke up early to get the car ready for the road trip to Pennsylvania. I heard Sam in his room crying softly. I went in to see him and sat down on the bed, gathering him in my arms. "What's up, buddy?" I asked. "You okay?"

"I want my daddy back," he said.

"I know it's hard that Daddy travels all the time," I said. "But we are all going away to have some fun together."

"I had a bad dream that Daddy left us forever. He went away!" he said sadly as his eyes filled with tears that spilled down his cheeks. My heart went out to him. I wondered whether this had anything to do with the transfer. The timing was so close, and Sam had never done anything like that before. I wondered whether right after the transfer, Tom had come to visit Sam in his dreams to say good-bye. I suspected this was true. It couldn't just be a coincidence – of course there is no such thing as a coincidence, everything happens for a reason.

The entire trip to Hershey Park was almost surreal. This was the first time since as far back as I could remember that my husband wanted to join in the fun and be happy. It seemed to be his mission. He went out of his way to be kind and make sure we all were comfortable. To my complete surprise, he even went on the Skyrush roller coaster with me. I loved roller coasters, and Tom would never go with me. "I just want you to have a good time!" he said when I asked him whether he was sure he wanted to join me. Yes, things were changing. The entire trip was wonderful.

Just a few days after we returned from the Hershey Park trip, we packed up again to meet Tom's family for our annual reunion on Block Island, something we had done for the past twenty years or so, since we were married. There was to be a lot packed into this short summer, it seemed.

After it all died down, a couple of weeks after we returned, I called April to give her an update on everything that had happened. She was in town, and we decided to meet for breakfast.

"So..." April asked. "Is he different?"

"Very," I said, smiling back from ear to ear.

"And..." she said.

"And yes, we made love. The very night you told me about the transfer."

"I'm so happy for you!" April said. "What a nice welcome back to earth for him."

"Oh, thank you. And for me too! It's so amazing that it even happened! It was not the same as when Jay and I were younger, naturally, but still...he *wanted* me, April. He *really wanted* me! I felt loved, more than I have been in years."

"How wonderful!" April said. In any ordinary conversation, the fact that two married people made love is not that newsworthy. But in this case, there was so much to it.

"I can't wait to tell you about the rest of the week!" I said excitedly. We were having breakfast at our favorite diner, Jigger's.

"Tell me," April replied, digging into her corned beef hash and eggs.

"Ok, but before I do, I wanted to let you know that I've decided to call this new husband of mine Jaymie. A combination of Jay and Tommie." I interjected.

"So he'll be Jaymie from now on? Tommie/Jay does seem a little cumbersome," April asked.

"Yes, I agree. I think Jaymie would work between you and me and the other few of us that know what's going on, which, as you know, aren't many. To everyone else, I guess he needs to stay Tom. Until he becomes awake and aware to what's happening. Then he'll be back to Jay, I hope."

"Perfect." April replied.

"So, it was quite a trip! We have been vacationing on Block Island for years, since we were kids. We were in the car on our way to the ferry, and Tom—now Jaymie—got completely lost. Missed the exit and didn't know how to get back. Now here's a guy who has been to this ferry a hundred times, and he just couldn't get there, simply could not find his way," I explained.

"Really?" April asked, although deep in thought.

"Yes. I did think it was odd, but I didn't know what to expect with the new Jaymie. Then, when we got to the island, he was in such a good mood and said, 'Let's rent some mopeds and take a spin around the island.'"

"Sounds like fun," April said.

"Yes, I thought so. I was thrilled with this new husband of mine! He actually wanted to do things!" I replied. "So we walked over to the moped rental kiosk and let them know we wanted two of them for a few hours. We had to show our licenses and go for a little test run to make sure we could handle the bikes."

"Handle a moped?" April asked. "Not too hard."

"I didn't think so," I said. "We both knew how to ride them. So I got on and got my bearings, went for a spin around the little parking lot, and waited for Jaymie to do his test run." I paused to take a bite of my spinach eggs Benedict and a sip of my juice. "The next thing I know is Jaymie is on the moped, revving it up. I looked over to him, and he was out of control on the bike, crashed into a little sign in a cement bucket, lost his balance, and fell off the bike!"

"Oh, no!" April said. We both laughed.

"It was funny, but of course not funny at the same time," I said through my laughter. "So the moped attendant had to tell him that they were not going to be able to rent a moped to him, since he couldn't handle the bike."

"Oh, that's funny," April said, laughing.

"So of course," I continued, "the joke for the weekend was that he lost his moped license. Here is a man who previously had a license to drive small cruise ships, not being able to handle a moped?" We both shook our heads, still giggling about it. "This had to have something to do with the transfer, don't you think?"

"Yes, I can almost guarantee that he is not fully seated into Tom's body yet. On the spirit side, they are taking their time with it, monitoring it very closely. Remember how the guide talked to us about how he would go back and forth a bit between the two personalities?" April interjected.

"Yes," I said. "I remember." Thinking back to that conversation.

"The concern was if Jay's soul infiltrated too fast into Tom's body, he could lose memories. On the trip to Block Island, it seems like this may have happened, and he did seem to lose some of Tom's memories. That was right after the transfer, wasn't it?" April asked.

"Yes, about a week after," I replied.

"Maybe it all happened too fast, and they needed to pull Jay's soul back a little, incorporate more slowly into Tom's body. They need Jay's personality to slowly intertwine with Tom's cellular memories in the body, because, remember, Jay wanted to support your family. He needed Tom's memories to do that, at least his job memories," April explained. "What happened on Block Island ties right into how and why the process has taken the course it has," she said. "There is a sense to it, a plan. This is why, as I told you before, you two are under a microscope from the spirit side. They are as much interested in the outcome as we are!"

"Okay, now I can see why they are being cautious with Jay and his full transformation into the body," I said thoughtfully. "There was such a huge change in his behavior. That night, it was so sweet. I was having trouble sleeping, and my whole body was buzzing with energy. Next thing I know, Tom has his arm around me from behind, snuggling me. He did it while he was fast asleep, somehow instinctually knowing I wanted to be held."

"Awww…" April replied meaningfully. She knew that up until the transfer, Tom would recoil from my touch, and how much that hurt me.

"I know!" I said. "It was so nice. The next morning, I woke up, and we were in the same position. It's been so long, and I was so happy."

April looked at me and smiled.

"And the entire weekend, he was kind, happy, loving. He was talking to total strangers, telling stories, laughing out loud, completely out of character. He wasn't obsessed with money. He was generous—generous with it so we could have fun. Even Tom's family, who we were with, noticed a difference. They all wanted to know why he was so happy, seemed so different. His brother-in-law said to me, 'He's so happy. What's going on with him?'"

"And that was just the beginning," April replied.

"Yes, only the beginning," I said, beaming.

41

JUNE CLEAVER BEADS

It was my birthday, and the family decided to make breakfast for me. Tristan is a wonderful cook, and it was a sweet gesture. I loved that they wanted to do something special. After we finished the buckwheat pancakes with big, fresh blueberries, thick-sliced bacon with a crispy glaze, scrambled eggs, fresh cantaloupe and strawberries, and maple syrup from a farm we visited in Vermont, we were stuffed. The kids started to take the dishes off the table and into the kitchen to wash.

Jaymie said to me, "I have something..." He got up and handed me a small gift that he had hidden on a shelf near the table. "This is for you."

"Oh, thank you!" I said, smiling at him. I opened the little blue box with the white satin bow, and inside was a lovely pearl bracelet. "This is beautiful!" I said, looking at him with affection.

"To match your June Cleaver beads," he said.

I couldn't believe my ears. Did he really remember those tender moments when we were younger? Then I opened the card, and there was the most beautiful poem about how important I was to him.

As I looked down at the signature, I noticed it was completely different. His signature seemed to look like Jay's handwriting, at least from what I could remember. Tom's handwriting was small, sharp, condensed, and severe. Jay's was bigger with big, open loops. Complete difference, and there it was, staring me in the face.

"Did you sign this card?" I asked him jokingly. Tom often signed his cards to me "From your husband, Tom." This one simply said "Love, Tom." Such a simple difference, but it meant so much to me.

"Of course I did!" he said, laughing. "Who else would?"

"No one," I said, smiling at him. "Thank you so much." I stood up and gave him a hug. "It's beautiful."

42

WORKING ON MYSELF

As I let things take their course and supported Jaymie with quiet anticipation, I became passionate about my own spiritual awakening. It became so important to me to understand as much as I could about the spirit world, how it worked, why things were the way they were, and how my little life story fit into it all.

I realized that I could do only so much with my earth mind and that if I just stayed happy, allowed things to unfold naturally, everything would be perfect—whether it was the "perfect" I expected it to be or not, it would all make sense in the long run.

I have come to believe that there are no accidents and everything works out exactly as it should—whether we think so or not. I just needed to have faith and go from trying to control the flow and outcome of just about everything to letting the outcome flow to me. Once I realized this and began working on myself and my personal actions and reactions, I began to experience a complete calmness and a whole new life. Everything that seemed to bother me before simply vanished. The things that worried me left.

As I stopped worrying about things and let events simply flow and take their natural course, my life became so easy. Prior to this change, I would try to control just about everything. I thought that control would keep me safe. Looking back, I realize it was just me in survival mode.

I knew I was hardworking and clever and wanted to use my gifts to make people happier, make things better for them, and help them be more successful. Unfortunately, as I found out, people usually did not need or want my help. They had their own lives to live, and lessons to learn. Those who did take the help I willingly offered, greedily squirrelled it away and seemed to appreciate none of it. This left me feeling foolish and used. I soon found out who the givers and the takers in my world were.

I finally got it that people's lives were none of my business nor mine to resolve. Even if I meant well, it was an intrusion. It was such freedom to know that it was not always up to me to make everyone happy. People had their own paths to follow, their own lives to live and lessons to learn. I needed to mind my own business and be very selective with whom I opened myself up to. Once I discovered this, life became a lot easier.

Since I was a child, even with all the madness of my home life, I always knew I had a sort of "powerfulness" although I couldn't really put my finger on what it was. I seemed to simply know things. Not the typical psychic abilities you may think of, but a simple, solid knowing. I knew how things would turn out; I knew how situations came about and why. I knew the real intention of people; and instantly whether a person was good or had ulterior motives. And I could usually tell when someone was lying.

I knew that if I worked on opening myself up more to my true spirit, spirituality, and the universe as a whole, it would be easier for Jay to settle into this world. I wanted to learn all I could. I didn't know what I didn't know, but I was open to finding out.

Through a referral, I made an appointment with Dr. Meredith. She was a psychologist who also worked with the spiritual world when opportunities arose.

I was both confused and fascinated by what was happening in my life and completely overwhelmed with how to deal with it. I needed someone to talk with about it all, and Dr. Meredith seemed a good place to start.

I wasn't sure what to expect on my first visit with her, but I very much wanted to better understand my past and how to deal with some of my issues that were holding me back, most specifically my feeling of unworthiness. Also, I wanted someone to talk with that wouldn't hold judgment about all the changes that were happening in my life and would be open to the spirituality of what was happening. I quickly found out that Dr. Meredith was the perfect choice.

"Tell me a little about yourself," Dr. Meredith said. "What brought you here today?"

"I'm trying to work my way through some things and was referred to you by some friends." I went on to say, "And they absolutely *love* you."

"Oh, that's so nice. Thank you for sharing that with me!" Dr. Meredith said sweetly.

I told her a little about myself, my background, and my childhood. My life in a fifteen-minute verbal essay. I mentioned to her that I was struggling with not feeling "worth it." I didn't understand why I felt this way all the time, and didn't understand why people were still attracted to me, wanted to be around me, and were asking me for help and telling me their life stories at our first meeting. "I don't get it. What do they see that I don't?" I asked her.

I could see at that first meeting why everyone thought so highly of her. She was deeply caring, smart, and completely unassuming. As we got to know each other, we talked, and she waited for any clues from me before she brought up spirituality. As a licensed psychologist, she was walking a fine line with her belief in spirituality and her strict professional standards. She did it beautifully.

Dr. Meredith gently said, "You have a lot of healing energy, angel energy. It's beautiful." I guessed that she had decided it was okay to bring up the spiritual side of things. Her statement was expressed to me with such love and kindness that I felt my healing was well on its way.

I told her about what was happening with my husband, the walk-in process. She listened intently, without a trace of judgment. She had

179

heard the term "walk-in" before, through the book *Strangers among Us* by Ruth Montgomery, but admitted she had not come across the situation personally or professionally. We talked about Jay being my soul mate and what that meant in the bigger picture of what was going on. She told me she believed Jay and I had lived many lives together.

"Have you thought about past-life regression?" Dr. Meredith asked.

"I've always been intrigued by it," I said. "Thought about it a lot, but not sure where to go or who to talk with about it."

"Well, I think it may be good for you to explore—get a better idea of why you are who you are. And it would be interesting to see if and when Jay was with you in other lives."

"Oh, that would be interesting," I said.

"I know a great person you can see to help you with it. Her name is Jackie," Dr. Meredith offered.

I jotted down the name and number on the back of an old business card I found at the bottom of my purse. "Thanks. I'll call her," I said.

I was sincerely trying to understand my spirituality on a deeper level. The situation with Jay opened up so many new thoughts and feelings, and I knew there was much more to this universe that I could explore.

After I made an appointment to see Dr. Meredith again, I walked out of the office, and humbly gave thanks and expressed my gratitude to the universe. "Thank you for bringing this woman into my life," I said to the sky. While driving away from her office that day, I knew it was going to be a wonderful relationship. Science with spirituality in perfect harmony—it didn't need to be one or the other. It was perfect together.

Dr. Meredith and I worked together for many months, and I learned some of my most profound lessons in sessions with her. I believe she was placed in my path for this reason. She was truly a gift to me.

43

ENOUGH ALREADY!

"I don't know who it is that I'm living with now, but I can tell you I don't want him!" I said to April, doing my best to hold back tears of complete frustration. "I've had enough! The whole situation is too much to handle. Tom is acting the same as he ever has when at his worst. Disrespectful, uncaring, mean, controlling, manipulative, screaming at the kids."

"Oh, boy, I can see you're upset," April said.

"It's like we went back to the way things used to be, before Jay was here. The wonderful man who was now my husband for the last six months seemed to disappear!" Since I had experienced the kindness and caring of Jay, the contrast to what I was feeling now was alarming. This man who was calling himself my husband was pressing my buttons, big time.

"Tell me what is happening," April said to me, trying to calm me down.

"I just don't believe all this!" I said. "If this is what it means to have Jay back, I don't want it!" I said, almost screaming to April on the phone. I was beside myself. "I don't know if Tom is back or if he is just interfering with us, but whatever it is, I want no part of it," I said, completely distraught.

"Now, take a deep breath," April said peacefully. "Jay is definitely here, but as we have been told from the other side, he's not fully incorporated into his earth body, not one hundred percent here yet."

"Well, he's being a dick," I continued. "You should have seen him tonight. We were at a restaurant having dinner, and he was so mean to the server. He was acting like a snob, talking down to her, an elitist pig, and making her feel small for being in a service position. Like somehow he was better than she, like she was stupid or something. She was just doing her job!"

I felt so strongly about this. Being in service, to me, was an honor. It didn't matter whether you were a server in a restaurant, a cashier in a grocery store, or a general in the army; to truly serve, to truly give of yourself, was an honor. It should be treated as such.

"Uh-oh..." April replied.

"When he was through with her, he started in on the kids and me. It drove me crazy, the kids were upset, and he set off every button that he knows how to press in me! He has this awful way of reacting to things you want to share with him or offer him in kindness, to make them sound like a stupid idea, something that you should be embarrassed to even offer," I continued.

"You've got to remember that it's only been a few months. Jay is still trying to get his bearings. Tom's soul is gone, but his cellular memory is still in his body," April reminded me. "I am hearing from the other side that you are responding to him as if he were still Tom. This is solidifying that behavior. Don't react to him. Let him rant and rave. The behavior will bubble up and then dissipate. This will give Jay's authentic reactions a chance to solidify."

I took a breath and collected my thoughts. "For these past few months, Jaymie has been wonderful and caring. We have shared some great moments that I cherish. It really seemed that Jay was back—even if it was hard to believe since everything else was Tom—his body, his gestures, his family and memories. Still, I know Jay was with me, and trying. I could live with that. I appreciate that." I paused and then continued. "I just want to make this as easy as possible for him, if there is any way that I can. I can only imagine how he must feel."

"It must be so difficult for him," April agreed.

I went on. "I know this is not an average situation that happens every day, but it seems that somehow Tommie is back, or just meddling somehow. Either way, I don't want it! It has been an incredible ride of ups and downs. I have tried to understand, stay open minded, act on the advice given from our guides on the spirit side, but this is it. I'm done."

April was quiet, waiting for my tirade to subside. When it finally did, she said, "Okay, again I'm getting from my guides that you need to not feed into the negativity. There are parts of Tom that are bubbling up. They need to dissipate. It's just a way for these memories and responses to leave his system. If you feed into them and fight back, these will then be the memories that Jay creates now as the new soul in Tom's body, and they will be solidified, learned responses," April explained. "And these are the memories you don't want, right?"

"Of course I don't want them! But I'm not sure I understand what you're talking about," I said to April, unsatisfied. This was not helping.

"We all have cellular memory in our bodies. Things we have learned over our lifetime, our memories, our responses. This cellular memory is not something we lose, and because Jay did not have a trauma or a near-death experience, he did not get a chance to reboot the body—to clean out the memories and start fresh," April explained.

"Okay, that makes sense, I guess," I replied.

April went on. "Remember this hasn't happened this way before from the spirit side. This situation is under a microscope in spirit, because it has bigger consequences. They are careful and experimenting with all this to make sure you are kept safe. Jay was adamant that he be able to support his new family in a way that would be safe, uninterrupted, and in a way that he felt you deserved. To do this, he had to retain Tom's memories, more specifically his work memories. We still don't know what of Jay's memories he may have had to sacrifice to do this."

"Well, we seem to be stuck with the memories we don't want!" I said, still distressed but trying to calm down. I wasn't thinking clearly and didn't fully understand the implications of all this; all I knew was that I didn't want this life back.

April paused. She seemed to be debating something with herself. She then said, "I didn't tell you at the time, but I was afraid of what Tom might do..."

"What are you talking about?" I asked, somewhat alarmed.

"My guides told me that when Tom got back to the spirit side, he didn't want to do his life review. On the one hand, he was happy that he didn't have to be here anymore, but then, when it sunk in that someone could take over his life and do a better job of it, it upset him. Add this to the fact that he was refusing to do his own life review because he would have to admit that his life wasn't perfect and you were so unhappy. I'm sure that must have kicked his ass," April explained.

"So he thought he got a free pass on his life review since he was part of this walk-in situation with Jay?" I asked.

"Yes, but I guess they made him do it finally, and he didn't like what he saw," she said. "They are also saying that Tom is not happy with how this all happened, and at the last minute he tried to back out. He thought it was a trick."

"A trick? I remember you telling me that when you called me about the transfer," I said. "After eighteen months of negotiations, a contract, and an agreement? He didn't have to agree to this, but he did."

"He did agree to it," April said. "He had to go through counseling on the other side because he was so upset. I hate to say this, but you deserve to know..." she added carefully. "He was plotting and planning how he was going to destroy the happiness you finally did have."

"Really? That's terrible. What the hell? Was his acting up today part of this?" I replied, getting very annoyed now at both Tom and April. I didn't like the fact that she had held this from me. "Why didn't you tell me?"

"Well, it was probably me guarding you from him. I was having a war with him, and he was really upset. The guides that worked with him making the transfer were also involved."

"When did this all happen?" I asked.

"It was months after the transfer happened, and you were settling into your new life and relationship," April replied. "Tom was having hissy fits, ranting and raving from the other side. He was mad that Jay was a better father, better at his job, doing all these great things to help you and the extended family. Tom tried so hard to be perfect at everything he did when he was here, and he couldn't understand how anyone could do his life better than he could."

I was upset and not just a little frightened. "So when you think about it, he was so spiteful and thinking, 'Sure I'll leave. I don't want to be here anyway, and screw what happens with everyone else!'"

"Most likely," April said. "But I don't think he thought the whole thing through. His negotiations proved that he was not interested in your being happy, because it's not that he wanted you; he just didn't want anyone else to have you." She paused. "That was the general consensus of what the guides were telling me, anyway."

"I didn't know it was that bad. How could I have not seen or understood this behavior when he was here?" I replied. "I think it's become pretty obvious that Jay very much wants to make this all work, and Tom never has."

"And then Jay was here, taking on Tom's role and responsibilities in so many ways—taking care of his mother, taking care of you. He turned out to be a great father and was even waking up early to make breakfast for everyone and drive Sam to school," April replied. "I remember you telling me that."

"Yes, that and so much more. He has been incredible, a perfect husband and father in so many respects," I interjected. "He has even made so many new friends. People like to be around him. That was never the case before."

"I'm sure Tom was thinking, 'How dare he be better at my life than I was!'" April said.

I laughed, thinking how ironic the whole thing was. "Oh, man..." There were so many life lessons in this situation.

April paused. "Can you imagine how that must have made him feel? He just dug his heels in because he thought it would be so much easier than this," she continued. "He comes from a long line of difficult men, I'm hearing from my guides."

"Yes, that sounds about right," I said, thinking about how bullheaded his father could be. Charming, yes, but also bullheaded and dismissive.

"My guides are telling me that Jaymie will start to sing," April said.

"Sing?" I repeated. Singing was something Jay often did when we were together, and something that Tommie would never think about.

"Yes, sing," she replied. "They want you to know that he will start to sing. This is how you will know it's really Jay that's here with you."

"Okay, but how will that get rid of this person I'm living with?" I knew I was being a brat, but I was overcome with frustration and pent-up anger, and I just didn't seem to know how to work through it anymore.

"It won't. They just want you to know this is just a small way you will be able to tell that Jay is truly with you. It's just a way to help you through this." April stopped. "I will work with your guides to see what we can do about this or see why it's happening."

"Okay, I'd appreciate that," I said, still not content.

"And in the meantime, I will make sure Tom is in lockup on the spirit side."

"Lockup?" I asked. "You can do that?"

"Yes, temporarily, until he calms down and stops interfering with you," she said. "There is a natural law that says no one is allowed to interfere with your free will. When and if someone does, you can ask for the person's privileges for communication with this earth world to be taken away until the person calms down and works through it."

"Really? How do you do that?" I asked.

"Simply state that so-and-so is interfering with your free will and you want their ability for communications to be taken away," she said. "It's not permanent. But it helps for the time being."

"That's a good thing to know," I said. I had a feeling I might need this info in the future.

"Yes, it is. You can also ask him to leave you alone. Just ask him directly, out loud or through your thoughts and intentions, to leave you alone. He's made his decision. Let him know how you feel about this. You have every right to."

44

THE HILLS ARE ALIVE

The next morning, we were sitting in the family room, having coffee and checking e-mail. Sam was sitting on the couch next to me, playing a video game. It was a quiet Sunday, and things were happy and peaceful, exactly how I loved them to be. This was turning into our new normal.

"Did you know how talented your dad is?" Jaymie said to Sam. Sam looked up with a sure-Dad-whatever-you-say smile that only an eleven-year-old can pull off and still be cute. Then he went back to his video game.

"The hills are alive," Jaymie belted out singing, "with the sound of music! With songs we have sung for a thousand years!" He was loud, awful, and off key, but it was the sweetest music I had ever heard.

"Nice, Dad," Sam said. "Keep your day job."

"Pretty good, huh? I guess you didn't know your dad was a great singer," Jaymie said to Sam.

"No, and I still don't," Sam replied, smiling slightly.

"I'm not sure how Julie Andrews would feel about it, but I thought it was great. You can sing for me anytime," I said and walked over and gave him a kiss on the cheek. He smiled at me, beaming.

"Touché. Nicely done, Jay. Thanks for the message," I said softly under my breath.

45

WHAT IS A LIFE REVIEW, ANYWAY?

April and I were sitting in the office of her spiritual center, talking before we began the reading. I had come up to New Hampshire with Katie, a friend and coworker who wanted to meet April and have a reading. I hadn't seen April in a few months, so we decided to take a ride up north to see her.

Katie was finished with her reading and came out of the small reading room.

"How did it go?" I asked her.

"It was good," Katie replied. "A lot for me to think about. Sometimes this stuff is hard to believe. I'll just have to wait and see." Katie was intelligent and practical. She was open to the spiritual side of things but wanted to mull over in her mind what she had learned in her reading before she made any determination as to its purpose or usefulness.

"Okay, I'm next. See you in a bit," I said as Katie put her earphones in to listen to the recording of her reading. She had some mulling to do.

"I have Tom's family here..." April said a few minutes after we sat down as she connected to spirit. "It's on his father's side. They want to thank you for how well you treated Tom while he was here. They know he wasn't good to you in many ways, and they appreciate what you did for him."

"Oh, that's nice," I said. "It's amazing to me how they know so much on the spirit side."

"They also want you to know that they have given Tom something to do on the other side so he can calm down, learn to deal with his decisions, and leave you and the family alone," April reported.

"Thank heavens!" I said. "It is amazing to me that they can watch over us from the other side. Know what's going on in our lives." I giggled. "It's kind of creepy in a way, if you think about it."

We both laughed.

"I'm just kidding." I went on. "I have a wonderful friend and medium, Holly, who explained it to me once. She told me that if they are not around you, they are always available to you," I said, smiling. "You can call out to them, and they can come at an instant's notice—if they want to, of course—but they can't be in two places at once. Some will stay with you more often; some will pop in and out. I guess it just depends how spiritually or mentally close to you they feel."

"Right," April replied. "And also, it's really interesting to me that once you die, you hear and you know how everybody felt about you. Good, bad, or indifferent, you know," April said. "You can accept some of it, and I'm sure you don't want to believe some of it."

"What happens with your life review anyway? Is it that we see how everything we have done affected others while we were here?" I asked. This was a question I had always wondered about.

"First, to look at what you did with your life, what you expected to do with your life, and how close you got to those expectations," April stated.

"Umm, yes, okay," I said. "And how you affected others with what you did?" I interjected.

"The second part is to find out why people feel the way they do about you," April continued. "And some simply do not want to hear it. For some people, denial is not just a river in Egypt."

We both laughed.

"How many people do you know that know they should change but defend themselves as to why they do what they do instead of changing their behavior?" April asked.

"Lots, of course," I said. "Okay, but what if somebody is defending something they did and there are opposite opinions on it?" I was thinking about how strong some people's opinions can be and why they hold to them with steadfast conviction, despite the fact sometimes those opinions and convictions obviously aren't serving them.

"That is sometimes why people have to come back around and live that lesson again," April said. "Because they didn't understand it the first time around, or refused to see it."

"Ummm, yes," I said. That was a little epiphany for me.

"It's like taking a math test and failing it, taking it again and getting fifty percent, and the third time getting one hundred percent. Your denial or mediocrity means you must do it again, learn it in another life. See what I'm saying?" April asked.

"I do," I said, thinking this was insight into a bit of karmic law.

"It's just a process. There is no judgment on the other side, other than the fact that what you do to others you have to make amends for, at some point," April continued. "The end goal is for us to become equal with God. It's not the plan on the other side for us to be hurt or abused or wounded to learn a lesson. We do that all by ourselves. The spirit world doesn't get involved in that part of it," April said. "But there are things we have to learn."

"There certainly are," I said, thinking just how much more there was available to learn. The possibilities to learn and grow are all around us. We just have to open ourselves up to them.

46

MORE THAN I BARGAINED FOR

I turned into the driveway and pulled around back to park my car in front of the garage. I was on my way in to see Jackie for a spiritual reading. I had been to her a couple of months before to learn about some of my past lives, and what I found out was interesting. Jay and I had been in lives together before this one. He looked different, as did I, but there was no mistaking whose soul it was. It seemed Jay and I had been together for many lives on earth.

I was thinking how interesting this meeting would be. I loved Jackie's style; she was direct and got right to the point, while she was very caring in her mediumship messages.

I entered the light and bright space where she met with her clients. "How pretty," I thought. I said hello to Jackie with a big hug, and we embraced warmly.

"It's so good to see you again," Jackie said to me. "Did our last session help you?" she asked.

Our last session had been a past-life regression, which really helped me to get over my fear of heights, among other things.

"Yes!" I said. "It's amazing how that works. How something from a past life can affect you so deeply in this one." Until then, unless I was securely fastened into a roller coaster or something similar, I had been deathly afraid of heights and never understood why—but now I did and was thrilled that the sick feeling in the pit of my stomach when I was anywhere that took me more than two feet off the ground was gone.

I didn't have anything specific I wanted to talk to Jackie about or to ask of the spirit world, but I did have a list of questions I wanted to explore.

"Sit down. Make yourself comfortable," Jackie said to me.

I glanced at Jackie and thanked her as I looked around to find a spot to get comfortable. Since I was a little girl, I had been on the chubby side—and that chubby little girl grew into a plus-sized adult who was not always comfortable in her own skin. I didn't overeat—too much—but as a former chef and restaurateur, I did appreciate and love good food. My idea of a great time was to have dinner at a Michelin three-star restaurant. Still, I never understood how this could turn me into a large woman. I blamed it on my big bones, which even I didn't completely believe. I was constantly on the go, worked hard, and never sat around eating bonbons, watching television.

"I have questions," I said to Jackie.

"Okay," she said. "Would you like me to connect with spirit first? Or start there?"

"Why am I overweight?" I blurted out with a little too much eagerness. I didn't know where that question had come from, apart from the fact it was on my mind just about every day. "Oops, sorry. I didn't mean for that to come out so fast—it wasn't even a question on my list..." I explained as I blushed, embarrassed. That Celtic curse of mine—every time I showed emotion or had a cocktail, the very fair skin on my face and neck turned red. It was very easy to read my emotions. Needless to say, I was terrible at poker.

"Do you really want to know?" she asked, looking at me intently.

"Seriously? Of course I do!" I said eagerly.

I questioned whether this woman actually had a simple answer as to why I was overweight, but didn't think it could be that easy. My weight was something I had been trying to come to terms with my entire life. It was something about me that had caused me to deal with those sometimes-obnoxious people who felt superior and sorry for me at the same time, saying things like "You have such a pretty face. Have you tried to lose weight?" or the standard "You just need to get a bit of exercise. It will come right off." Ugh. Really, guys? This was so insulting, especially to someone who swam four times a week. Still, there it stayed, on my hips, belly, and butt.

I have never understood why the appearance of a person matters so much as to how they are perceived and judged. Who are any of us to judge another anyway? We are all different. We all look different. This is what is so great about the diversity of people in our world. Who wants to look the same or be the same? Get to know the inside, and then determine your thoughts about a person.

"All right, I'll tell you," Jackie said, looking at me seriously. "You're an earth angel."

I looked at her with a blank stare. I was not comprehending.

"Yes," she said, smiling at me, noticing the blank look on my face. "Your weight is there to protect you."

I continued to stare at Jackie in disbelief. I blinked a couple of times, trying to gather my thoughts and wrap my head around what she was saying.

Jackie continued. "You are very sensitive to most things, people, and circumstances. It is there to protect you from the negative vibrations around you. Protect you from the people who are on a lower vibrational level than you."

"Oh," I replied, completely dumbfounded.

"Many earth angels have body image issues," she continued. "Not all do, but many."

"So there are others like me? I just never thought..." I said.

"Of course!" Jackie said. "Many. Earth angels, light workers, indigo children. You were put here, or maybe asked to come here, to help the vibrational shift of the population. It is an honor to do this work." She continued, "I knew the minute you walked in you were an earth angel. I could see your wingspan. It's beautiful, and it could take up this whole room."

Now I was open to most things, but this was a lot for me to take in and process. For someone who felt completely unworthy to be roaming around the earth, feeling that I didn't measure up to those around me, to hear something like this was a shock. Albeit a happy shock. All at once I felt peace, happiness, relief, and a strong validation. There was a reason for this little life of mine. I was here to help! The thought of that made everything seem right and fall into place.

Jackie went on to explain, "We are light workers. We're here to help, no matter how small, with the changes our population is going through with a shifting consciousness. There are many of us in the world."

I could feel so many possibilities opening up. I wanted to find out everything I could about light workers and earth angels. I wanted to understand my mission, why I was here, what my purpose was for this life, what I could do to be in service, and how I could be better and make a difference. *This* made sense to me.

"One of the things you have to make sure you do is to ground yourself," Jackie continued. "As an earth angel, you are constantly attracted to lightness and often find it hard to stay grounded in this world," she said.

I thought back to a morning ritual Dr. Meredith showed me how to do and, when I was awake enough each morning to remember, I did. It was for the same purpose of grounding myself into this world.

"What exactly does it mean to be grounded? How does that help?" I asked.

"Being grounded is staying in the present. Staying in the now. Paying attention, not being on autopilot." She paused. "It can create a balance between the physical world and the spiritual, which could be very helpful to you with everything you are going through."

"That sounds wonderful," I said. "What do you suggest?" I asked.

"Put rocks in your pocket," she replied. "It will help you stay grounded. Black tourmaline and obsidian work well, and so does carnelian."

I laughed and said, "Easy enough." I didn't need to hear that again. What could be more practical? Something as simple as putting rocks in my pocket would help me assimilate all the life changes, information, ideas, and concepts that were coming at me day after day. Perfect.

47

HOW DID HE KNOW?

April and I had developed a deep friendship. There were things going on in our spiritual lives that were almost impossible to talk about in detail with anyone else.

"I wonder how Jay knew to do this. That it was possible," I said one day, thinking out loud.

"He must have investigated it," April said. "It will be interesting when he finally does wake up to learn how much he actually knows about the other side."

"I know. I can't wait," I replied. "It is going to be so interesting to talk with him about all this when I finally can. I keep wondering how long it is going to take."

"I do too," April said. "They are giving us as much information as they can, or as they think is appropriate. I'm so grateful to be a part of the inside story of this," she said.

As usual, the conversation rolled around the situation we were both fascinated by, Jay becoming a walk-in to Tom's body.

"You know," April began, "there was a time I wouldn't have believed this. I would not have trusted it either. If it wasn't for the fact that I was presented with information along the way that actually proved to me that this was possible, I probably would not have been in a place for you to allow Jay to come through to you like he did."

"I think it is pretty interesting that you and I ended up meeting, and the circumstances around it. There are no accidents," I said to April. "I think you were specifically chosen to be the communication channel with this."

"Well, I'm pretty honored to be involved in the whole thing. I think it may be because I have been exposed to it, and I don't just believe what spirits from the other side say to me. They have to prove what they are saying to me somehow, to show me that they are being authentic. With Jay, there was such a peace I knew it was true instantly. I could feel it."

"And then the story unfolded. And here we are," I said.

"And here we are." She responded. "There are lots of cases of walk-ins, but none like this," she said.

"Yes," I said. "I researched the phenomenon quite a bit. This does seem a bit out of the ordinary, but growing."

"Up until now, in the walk-in process, there has always been a situation where there was a crisis. A person asking to leave." April went on. "A suicide or near-death experience. The universe or God—if that's what you choose to call it—is responding to that. Allowing the soul to leave the earth and allowing someone who wants to walk the earth to take over. The spirit side understands that this person can't handle the earth anymore or just wants to go home—back to spirit."

"Sometimes I guess it can just be too much for some to bear," I interjected. "There is such a denseness to living on the earth in physical form."

"Yes, it's very dense," April continued. "But here, the difference is that someone that loves you so much decided to go and find out if he could change places with your husband's body. If it hadn't been for Jay's persistence on the other side, none of this could have happened."

"That sounds just like Jay. The whole thing is so amazing," I said to April, thinking how grateful I was to have this incredible love story happening to me and to have him back to continue our lives together.

48

GOD, WE NEED TO TALK

I was getting ready for work on Friday morning, trying to think of ways that I could help Jay somehow. I wanted to be more effective to help him wake up to his situation, if it was possible. In the months that had passed after the transfer, I was told though mediumship sessions to let Jay awaken on his own, at his own pace—to let him progress naturally. I was so eager to "have my Jay back" that I looked for any clue that would seem to be different in his actions, demeanor, words, or thinking. It was slow going.

The time it was taking, as well as my not being exactly sure what I could or should say to him, was grating on my nerves and slowly wearing away my patience. What I seemed to have for a husband was a mix of Jay and Tom. He was much happier than Tom; he was funny and kind, laughed, and was more outgoing. And the tone of his voice really did change. It was not as nasal; it didn't have the annoying pitch that sometimes made my teeth grate. Tom had trouble pronouncing many words, which was no longer happening. He also could hear me, all the time. He seemed to no longer be hard of hearing – his left ear was working just fine.

It was so confusing because all Tom's mannerisms, sayings, and thoughts, and many of his habitual ways of doing things, were still in the cellular memory of this body. I wanted so much to talk to Jay as Jay. I dropped hints and began talking more openly about my own spirituality and some of the things I was doing, thinking about, and experiencing in hopes it might trigger something in him.

It was lonely. I felt as if I was carrying around a huge secret, and there were not many people with whom I could have a frank conversation about it. I mostly kept it to myself, talking about it with only a couple of people that were enlightened enough to understand and be open to the possibility.

As I was unlocking the door to my office, Bells, one of my friends and coworkers, strode into the office in a whirl of happy energy. She gave me a big hug and said, "How is the best broker in the world today?"

"I'm great," I replied, saying the words but not really feeling it.

"Nope. You're not great. What's up?" she said with a piercing look. Bells had a way of getting right to the point, and nothing got by her. No bullshit allowed in her world. It's one of the things I loved the most about her.

"Oh, I don't know. I'm just having husband issues," I replied.

"Well, I can't help you there," she said. Bells had never been married and wasn't planning on it anytime soon. She was a free spirit, intelligent and in tune, and lived life on her terms. "Take me or leave me" was a favorite line of hers.

"Let's grab a coffee and talk." She took my arm, and we went off to the little kitchen in the corner of the office.

"I don't know what is the matter with me. I just can't seem to shake this sadness," I confessed.

"About what?" she asked.

"I'm not sure..." I started, but I really did know. Jaymie was acting strangely. In the process of going from a bitter, mean, always-had-to-be-right kind of person, to a kind, caring, and loving man who now seemed only to want to make his family happy...something was wrong. He seemed to be stuck somehow, reverting back to his old ways.

"Well, what would the answer be if you did know?" she asked.

I reminded myself how much I appreciated our friendship. "Well, it's a long story."

"I've got time and coffee, so shoot."

"Well, did I ever tell you what was happening with my husband?" I asked. I was apprehensive to talk about what was happening at home with my "husbands," but Bells and I had a connection, and we had spoken at great length about spirituality before. I didn't feel as though she would be uncomfortable with my little saga, and I had to talk with someone else about it; I was ready to burst.

"Have you ever heard of a walk-in?" I asked.

"Don't think so," she replied.

"Well, a walk-in is sort of a soul transference. It is when one soul leaves the body and another soul takes its place."

"Nope, I have definitely not heard of that," she said.

"Well, it often happens in near-death experiences or when someone is injured and is in a coma. It's a way for one soul to leave the body and go back home to spirit, and another takes its place here on earth."

"Wow, that's cool," she said. "What about it?"

"Well, my husband is one," I stated. Now Bells had an open mind, but I wondered how she would take the bombshell I just dropped.

"Really," she said. She had met my husband only a couple of times, and she didn't know him before he became Jaymie, so she never would have noticed one from the other. "Tell me more."

I began to unravel the story for her and laid it all out and gave her most of the details. She was silent and watched me intently as I jabbered on.

"That is frigging amazing!" she said when I was finally done telling my story.

I was relieved to hear her reaction. I had never talked to anyone else about it, but I trusted Bells.

"Oh, my God, I've got chills!" she said as she rubbed her arms. "That is the most incredible love story I have ever heard!" She went on to say, "What that man who truly loved you did for you! What he went through to be back here with you."

"I know. Sometimes it's hard to believe myself," I replied.

"But why are you so bummed right now? Are things not working out?" she asked.

"I don't know. It seems that Tommie is rearing his ugly head again, and I'm just not sure how to handle it…" The more I talked about it aloud with Bells and shared my feelings, the more real it felt. It was great to think about, but saying it aloud in everyday conversation seemed to solidify it in this world as well.

"It's all wonderful, but I can't imagine what you are going through. Your whole world must seem upside down. Better, but upside down nonetheless," she added.

"Yes, exactly. The thing is I just don't seem to know how to talk to him now. I have to pretend he's still Tom until he becomes awake and aware, or I will set off all kinds of red flags and could be harmful to the awakening process he is on. I can't openly talk about this with him, but I so want to!"

"I get it. It can't be easy," Bells replied.

"But at the same time, I need to slowly offer thoughts and ideas to him that may trigger Jay's responses," I continued. "I feel like I'm on a tightrope doing a balancing act and my shoes are slippery!" I said, deflated. "I'm so afraid that I'm going to say the wrong thing, do the wrong thing, and mess it all up! And I just don't know what else to do."

"Oh, you poor thing, you need a hug," Bells said as she got up and came over to embrace me. "You're doing a great job. I know it's hard, but I don't know of any other person that could handle this as well as you are. So you're having a bad day—it's bound to happen with all this going on. Give yourself a break already."

"Thanks, Bells," I said. This woman always knew how to make me feel better.

"Let yourself be upset for another couple of hours, and then move on," she advised. Things were so simple and straightforward with her. She was a great friend.

"Okay, okay," I said, smiling at her. But I did think I would need more than a couple of hours to sort this all out.

Later that night, the loneliness and frustration overtook me, and I was enraged by the fact that I didn't know whom I was married to anymore; I didn't know what to do or how I could help. I was especially frustrated by the fact that I didn't know how to talk to him.

I had an argument with Jaymie about something completely ridiculous, like washing the dishes, and I stormed out of the house. I jumped into my car and raced down the highway with the warm wind whipping through the open windows. I didn't know where I was going; I just wanted to get away. It was a summer night, and I found myself at Narragansett Beach. It was long after dark, and there were only a few cars in the beach parking lot. I loved the smell and sounds of the beach, and at night it was so peaceful. There was a full moon shining on the water.

I was fuming, tired, and distraught and just wanted to unload my thoughts and feelings on anyone or anything. I parked my car and got out and walked straight down to the water's edge with determination. I took my shoes off and flung them toward my car angrily as I began screaming at the sky.

"Okay, God, what do you want from me?" I shouted into the ether. "I just don't know what else I can do. Show me what I can do to help!" I was sobbing at this point and began walking down the length of the beach with purpose, as though I actually had a destination. As I marched down the expanse of the beach in my bare feet, the water felt cool, and the bottom of my long, flowing skirt was drenched. I didn't care; I walked and walked, asking God for guidance, at the same time letting him know just how I felt about all this. "I'll do whatever I can to help him!" I yelled through my tears. "But I just don't know how! I don't know what to do!" I continued walking, trying to calm down. I felt so useless in my situation. I didn't know who my husband was anymore. "I just don't understand what's real anymore!" I screamed. "Please help me!"

As I calmed down and the tears began to subside, I thought about Jaymie and what he must have been going through as well. He must have felt so strange, knowing on some level that things were different, although he still had the same day-to-day life. He must have been so confused as he slowly went through this awakening process. We all acted as if nothing really had changed, although Jaymie and I were much closer. I needed to let him wake up on his own, but we were about three years into this transfer, and it seemed as if we were not really moving forward any longer, almost as if we were stuck. I understood intellectually that Jay was not going to one day wake up in Tom's body and say, "Hey, Carolyn, how have you been? It's been a long time. Let's go into the bedroom." But still...

After I finished storming up and down the beach, expressing my thoughts and feelings to the ether, I brushed the sand from my feet, climbed into the car, and drove home. I was completely drained. When I was finally home, I pulled into the driveway and could see Jaymie waiting for me through the window. He wasn't mad; he wasn't worried; he just wanted to talk. He came over to me, sat down next to me on the couch, and held me close.

This reaction to the argument was all Jay. He just wanted to talk, to work it out gently and with understanding. As I cried in his arms, I realized how much Jay had progressed, how much these reactions and responses were his own. I might not have been able to talk with him one-on-one at that point as though he were completely Jay, but I had so much of him back; my loneliness began to subside.

I could wait. I would wait. He was worth it.

49

FIRST GLANCE

I planned a dinner party for eight of my closest friends, and April was going to join us, followed by readings for my friends. It was a Friday night, and Jaymie would be coming home from the airport around ten. I told him about the party and asked whether he would like to join us. He declined and told me to make sure we all had a great time.

As I prepared the dinner, I was wondering what it would be like for Jaymie to see April. They had not seen each other since before the transfer, and at that time, Tom wanted nothing to do with her. I think her mediumship and psychic abilities scared the hell out of him, and he didn't know how to react to her. He believed in nothing spiritual; if he couldn't see it, hear it, or feel it, it didn't exist. He was not about to start researching the possibilities either. I remember him telling me once that he didn't believe in ghosts, because he had never seen one. I argued that he hadn't seen Japan either but it was still there. It was lost on him.

I was happy with how the dinner turned out. I loved coming up with recipes and menus to prepare for my friends. For this dinner, I decided to roast a whole beef tenderloin coated in caramelized shallots, crushed peppercorns, coarse sea salt, fresh chopped garlic, thyme, and flat-leaf parsley. I served it with a port-wine reduction and long-cut fingerling potatoes roasted with the tenderloin. We had hot popovers fresh out of the oven with Irish butter. I also served a spinach-and-poached-pear salad with gorgonzola. For dessert, we had a lemon-mousse torte also made from scratch and served with a three-berry sauce.

As we sat at the dinner table having dessert after the readings, everyone was sharing stories and fascinations about what they had learned. We were a tight group of friends who were very much into spirituality and enjoyed one another's company immensely.

Just after ten o'clock, Jaymie walked in the front door and exclaimed, "It smells great in here!" He put down his suitcase and said hello to everyone. He was happy to be home, even if his dining room was filled with a noisy, rowdy bunch of women. April was at the end of the table opposite me and turned around to face Jaymie. I saw him look directly at her and smile; recognition seemed to flash across his face. It was not the usual scowl he greeted her with. He paused for a moment and then took a second look at her. He seemed to fumble for a moment to regain his composure. It was odd.

He excused himself and went upstairs to put away his suitcase and get out of his tie and put on some comfortable clothes.

As the guests were leaving, I said to Jaymie, "I saved you some dinner."

"Great, thank you. I had a light dinner on the plane, but nothing compared to what you created," he replied. "I would love some."

I was wondering whether I had heard that right. Just another clue to Jay's presence. Complimenting my food, appreciating the fact that I had created something special—it was nice.

Later that night, while April and I sat by the fire taking part in one of our marathon conversations, exploring the meaning of all this and the incredible possibilities it held, April said to me, "Did you see the look on his face when he saw me?"

"Yes, he seemed to pause when he looked at you," I responded.

"It was an instant recognition. The second he saw me, I could tell he recognized me from the spirit side, since we communicated so often. Then his earth mind kicked in, and it was gone."

"Really? You think he actually recognized you from talking with his spirit on the other side?" I asked.

"Yes, I do," she said. "Do you remember during one of our readings, he told me he couldn't wait to meet me and that he was going to remember me? He was given permission to remember me."

"I think so," I replied. "But given permission by whom?"

"That I'm not sure about. Maybe it was the Council or whoever gave him permission to do this from the other side. Well, that man I saw in that instant was not Tom. It was Jay," April continued. "Tom wouldn't even look me in the eye before."

"I remember," I said to April. "He is so different, especially in his reactions to me, just in day-to-day communication. He's supportive and complimentary and even likes playing with the dog."

"Nice," April said. "That's proof that things are changing. The unfolding will take its own pace and its own path as Jay slowly seats into Tom's body."

"Well, it's all great, and I can wait," I replied. "I am just not sure what it is I am waiting for. It's kind of interesting that this same body I have been married to for years has a completely new personality. A personality that seems to get stronger every day."

"The new Jay?" April asked.

"The new Jay," I replied, smiling.

50

SEDONA

I was visiting Sedona for the first time, and while walking around the town, I came across a shop with an incredible array of stones, crystals, rocks, salt lamps, and many other spiritual items. It had a wonderful feel to it. I was drawn in and noticed I could get a reading.

"Hello," I said to the woman who was walking around the store, helping customers and answering questions. "I would like to schedule a reading, please."

"Of course. Come this way, and I will look at Alex's schedule. I can get you in at three o'clock, in about twenty minutes," she said while looking at the schedule online.

"Perfect, thank you," I said to the woman.

"Okay, in the meantime, feel free to look around a bit," she offered.

I began to peruse the myriad of things for sale, many I had never seen before. It was a great learning experience. I was so interested in all things metaphysical and spiritual and had been for years.

I stood over the huge display of healing crystals. I picked up an obsidian snowflake and held it in my hand. It was dark charcoal gray in color, with lighter-gray markings on it that really did look like snowflakes around the edges. Inside each "snowflake" was a lighter marking of gray as well. It felt cool and strong in my hand.

"Stone of purity and perseverance. Brings beauty, purity, and balance to body, mind, and spirit. Provides protection, brings peace of mind, and helps detoxify the body," the little card attached to the pouch holding a single stone explained.

"Perfect," I thought to myself. There are hundreds of varieties of stones, and each one can heal in different ways. And to combine them can create healing for anything specific. The possibilities are endless.

Then I picked up a rose quartz. It was a lovely light pink with ribbons of lighter pink, almost white. "Stone of Gentle Love," the card in the pouch read. It was used for gently soothing the heart and opened one for love, peace, and tranquility, inviting self-love. The card went on to announce that it eased pain, tension, cuts, bruises, and emotional wounds.

I didn't have any cuts or bruises to heal, but the part about easing the pain, tension, and emotional wounds seemed right up my alley. I had been having trouble with some of the agents in my real estate brokerage and had been wondering whether the real estate industry was for me. I knew it well, I was good at it, but at times the negativity and cutthroat practices were too much. After eighteen years in the business, I was getting tired of it all. I didn't want to play the game anymore.

I had tried to run the office with support, caring, mentoring, and kindness to all my agents. I was on a personal mission to try to change the nastier parts of the industry, or at least my little piece of it. It seemed to me that if I created a space of mentorship, openness, transparency, and professional kindness, it would be well received. And in the beginning, it was. We grew at an alarming rate. But after a few years, I had grown tired of the kill-or-be-killed recruiting practices to keep agents in my office. It was just not me, and I didn't want any part of it. It was time to enter the next phase of my life—I just didn't have any clue what that was.

This was one of the reasons I had come to Sedona. I booked the trip to go to a retreat with Gregg Braden and Dr. Joe Dispenza. I was looking forward to getting away by myself and figuring out what was next for me. How I could give back, heal, and help if I didn't have a direction or an occupation to do it in?

Wandering around, I felt happy in this place; it was light, bright, airy, and peaceful, and the people that ran the shop were helpful and professional. And it was charged with energy. I could feel it all over.

When I asked the purveyor of the shop what crystals would be good for me, as I had recently found out I was an earth angel, she gave me a knowing look and gently said, "Let's see what I can find for you." No judgment, no strange looks, just kindness. No wonder so many people loved Sedona, especially if they were exploring their spirituality or on their way through the awakening process. Everyone here seemed to understand. It was their way of life.

The woman came back with samples, and she showed me what she had picked out for me. I listened intently. I chose a few stones and asked her to hold them for me at the register.

"Oh, it looks like it's time for your reading," she said as she ushered me into the private room in the back of the shop.

"Thank you very much," I said as she opened the door.

"Hi, I'm Alex," the young woman who was there for my reading said. She seemed very businesslike, and we got right to it. "Please sit down. What brought you in for a reading today?" she asked.

"I was walking around the town and was drawn here, so I decided to come in for a reading," I said to Alex. That was true, but I also was interested in seeing whether another medium would channel either Tom or Jay, or both, from the spirit side. I wanted to see another's take on it, and l was looking for validation that I wasn't crazy or making more of the walk-in situation with my husband than what was actually there. To me, this life I was living—the situation, the coincidences, and what I saw and felt on a daily basis—was so real. But I did realize how it sounded to anyone outside of this belief. It sounded pretty strange.

"Okay, right on," she started. "Well, all mediums do things differently and have different flavors, and my flavor is that I work with intuition. Not just my intuition but your intuition too. We work as a team. So what I do is I pull out what the heart has to say. I want to make the most out of this time. What would you like to know?"

"Um, boy, I didn't come in with an agenda, so let's see where this takes us," I replied, but secretly I did have an agenda. It was Jay. "I guess I'd like to know more about my being here on the earth, my purpose," I said.

"Well, you are an earth angel," Alex stated. Boom, just like that.

I felt sheer happiness and validation. Peacefulness. Much like the first time I had heard this from Jackie and Dr. Meredith. I was finally connected.

"Do you know what an earth angel is?" Alex asked. "Have you heard this before?"

"I've been told I am an angel a few times before," I replied.

"Okay. Yes, you are an earth angel. You are very connected to nature, natural things: the earth, water, and gardens. As an earth angel, which is one of God's teammates, you are here to protect the earth and maintain balance. Water, earth, plants. You would make an excellent herbalist or naturopath. If you ever wanted to get into the homeopathic field, it would be a great place for you. These would be great things for you to study. Become certified. You can easily get a job doing this."

"Where am I supposed to be? What am I supposed to be doing?" I said, not really hearing what she was trying to tell me.

"Naturopath," Alex said.

"Also, I am trying to find out about my husband, who is a walk-in," I replied.

"Hmmm," Alex replied without missing a beat. She continued, "One of the things you are also here to do is balance emotions. When you are an earth angel, you are also empathic. Do you know what it means to be empathic?"

"Yes," I said. This I was well aware of.

"Okay, so you know what it feels like to walk into a room and take on everybody's *stuff*. And you do that, and you carry it, and you carry it so close to your heart because you are actually and naturally trying to heal it. But you don't know how to heal it, so it stays there. And you carry it around, and it becomes heavy on you. It pulls you down;

it drains your energy out. Makes it harder to deal with more," Alex explained.

"Absolutely. I can feel that heaviness, and it's draining all the time," I said to Alex.

Alex continued. "You need to learn what this means and how to deal with this. It is also called codependency."

"Oh, brother," I thought. "Not the codependency thing again." I had heard myself described this way for years. I never completely understood it or why it was such a bad thing. I thought of myself as just someone who wanted to be happy, help people, and help other people to be happy as well. How could that not be a good thing?

"This is what people do when they share their emotions. You take those emotions on, and they stay with you. You're trying to heal them without realizing it. And being codependent, you take on their baggage. And you do it with a glad heart. The problem with this is that it weighs you down and drains you. You need to live your own life, not just be there for everyone else," Alex went on.

As Alex explained this to me, it was beginning to sink in just how very codependent I had been for the first fifty years of my life. I always came last in my mind—everyone else's needs came first. Husband, kids, coworkers, friends—especially friends. Looking back, I saw that I seemed to attract people in my life that either needed fixing or wanted something from me. And I was happy to give it to them; it made me feel as if I was helping, and complete. I also felt that if I didn't help them, they would leave me. I wondered why anyone would need friends who treated her that way, but apparently, I did. But I was getting better; over the past few years, I had taken on an "I don't give a rat's ass what anyone else thinks about me" attitude. It worked, most of the time. Codependency was a hard habit to break.

"I did, and still do this sometimes. Less and less, but it is still there," I replied as if trying to prove this to myself as well as Alex. "I feel like I have gotten past this and have stopped the codependency. Or at least have it under control and am working to get rid of it daily. It's a work in progress."

"Okay, great," Alex said, continuing with her thought. "You do have a choice coming up if you want to enter the holistic field or natural medicine. But it is a choice. We have been given free will. This is one thing that God and the angels give us. You are allowed to say no," Alex continued. "This is an area where you are a natural healer. This is what you were born to do."

"It doesn't feel right," I said. I was so confused as to what I was supposed to be doing.

"What doesn't feel right?" Alex asked.

"All this employment stuff. I'm not here to find a job. I have a purpose, and I'm having trouble finding out exactly what it is. I just want to know my purpose!" I could feel my face growing red with frustration—the Celtic curse again, I thought. "People come to me constantly, and it drains me. Lately I don't really know how to help them!" I continued.

Alex continued patiently; she could tell I was upset and stuck. "Employment means purpose. You don't have to get a job. You can get a job or work in this area if you want to, or not. It is just your purpose. But it is also your choice."

I didn't know why this bothered me so much. This kind and obviously talented, spiritually connected woman was just trying to help, and I was being a bitch. Something was getting under my skin about all this. I wanted to figure out what it was.

"We all have a reason why we are on earth. You are employed by spirit. That's what they call karma. For you, it's to heal the earth. Keep it balanced."

I sighed and continued. "So I've been reading and studying what it means to be an earth angel. I'm trying to understand where I fit in. What I can do with it. I don't know why I need to know, but..."

"What do you feel connected with?" Alex asked.

"Helping. People are drawn to me in crisis. I just want to know what to do with it. I'm drawn more to people, not the earth as much," I replied.

"Aren't people part of earth?" Alex said.

"I hadn't thought of it that way. I think earth, physical, hard surface," I said.

"No, no, I'm not saying geologist, but you are helping people on earth. We are all on this earth together, so we're working together; we use all the resources together. We are all part of the earth, and you are here to heal and balance."

"I just want to help people be happy," I said. That part was very simple to me.

"Okay," Alex replied. "What makes them happy?"

"Being connected," I replied.

"Yes, but they think it is things," Alex countered.

"Oh, things...I can see where people may think that," I replied.

"Yes, most of the time, things." Alex went on. "Bigger house, more money, more vacation time, better connection with people. More, more, more."

"Oh, of course, but those things won't make you happy," I countered.

"No, they won't, but people have been coming into my office year after year after year, just wanting more. All they are really looking for is simplicity." I could see this was very important to Alex. "Okay, if you do not understand how you are connected with the earth, counseling is very much part of the earth. You're teaching people how to respect. How to respect themselves, how to be happy with what they have, and how to feel good and have simplicity. That's all earth-angel stuff," Alex explained, trying hard to get her point across.

"Okay! Now that feels right!" I said. "That makes sense to me!"

"Good, maybe I just needed to explain it a little differently to you," Alex offered.

"Yes, that totally feels right," I said.

"An earth angel is here to protect resources. We are all connected; we are all one. Helping others find simplicity, loving the earth, and protecting the earth." Alex went on. "It is just a different way of looking at things."

"Different is great. I love to look at things from a different perspective," I said to Alex, feeling some relief that this was all starting to make sense.

"Sometimes it might take a day or two to look at it all, research it, and find out how it's true for you. Think about the path you choose to take," Alex said, as we both laughed at the simplicity of a task that was so very overwhelming to me. It was that simple. Think about it, find out what was true for me, and make a decision on the path to take. I could do this.

"Follow what is true in your heart. Other people's opinions are just opinions, nothing more. Go with what resonates with you," Alex reiterated. "Counselor, perfect. Life coach, perfect. I may be jumping way ahead—I apologize," she said as she laughed. "I'm a psychic. I'll do that sometimes, you know? I'll see way into the future, and folks are like, 'Wait a minute. What's going on now?'" We both laughed; I appreciated her candor.

Alex looked at me warmly and said, "I'm giving you what I feel and what I see. I'm here to love you and give you what I see, in honesty and in honor. Because I care." Alex paused to think for a minute. "And I really do believe you are an earth angel. That is very clear to me. I have respect for you. You have a hard job on this earth. You are absolutely beautiful to me, glowing and radiant."

I looked at Alex as she said this, and felt the truth in her words.

"Let's talk a bit about your husband if you wish…" Alex continued.

I gave Alex an overview of the walk-in situation with Tom and Jay and where we were in the process.

"Oh, wow. Oh, wow…" Alex said quietly yet with interest. "Okay, let me see what comes through for you."

I was beginning to understand that the walk-in phenomenon was not one that most mediums came across every day. I was grateful that Alex knew enough about it to be open to exploring it with me a bit more. I could tell she was communicating with spirit.

"So…we're going to get a play-by-play…" she began, smiling.

"Oh, good!" I said. I loved to analyze all the details.

"When Jay was a walk-in and came into Tom's body, the first thing he had to do was reprogram the memories. There was the mind of Tom and the mind of Jay, and there are memories associated with each one. So Jay had to come in and plant the seeds of Jay. So there is a switch-off there. It can be a little hairy. It's literally like programming a computer," Alex explained.

"And it didn't help him that there was no accident or near-death experience, as often happens in these situations to clear out the memories," I offered. "There was no natural rebooting process."

"Exactly—right—it really took a toll. That is often how it happens with soul transference or as a walk-in," Alex agreed. "And this has been exhausting for him."

"I can only imagine what he has been going through. I'm sure it is very confusing for him internally. We are still in the process," I said to Alex.

Alex continued. "Sometimes Jay, because he is so powerful with you..." Alex trailed off. "He's your soul mate. Jay is your twin flame. That's rare. That is your other being of soul. That is your connection."

I smiled at her.

"There was still a part of Tom when this happened that didn't want to let you go. Tom sometimes wonders, 'Did I do the right thing?' He thinks about the things he wanted to share with you, the things he wanted to do with you and give to you, the love he had for you..." Alex paused. "And letting Jay come in—it just took that away from Tom."

"That's so nice to hear. I wish he could have shared that with me, but he didn't, or couldn't—I don't know which," I interjected, thinking that I was not going to let this send me down Guilt Trip Lane.

"Yes, he made his choice," Alex continued. "But there is still a little regret." She paused. "Especially since you are such a powerful being. So Tom—bless his soul—since he let it all go, still has some anger."

"Yes, he does!" I said with a laugh. "And we sometimes find that out the hard way."

Alex replied, "Because you are his family, *his* family. So now these two here, Tom and Jay, will have to deal with some karma when everybody goes back home to spirit. Because now really Jay is raising Tom's family."

"He is," I said. "And gratefully, we were privy to some of the negotiating process on the other side, how they negotiated and the contracts that they had to draw up. It was fascinating to learn about."

"Whoa," Alex said lightly. "What an unconventional family life! So this is more of a reading from Tom. It's mixed. You had a message for Jay, but Tom came through. Tom is saying he will give you your space, even though he has this feeling of regret. He is saying, 'I understand. I will give you breathing room. I'm okay with myself. I made the choice.'"

"Oh, good," I said, "I'm glad he is at peace with his choice." No matter what, I didn't wish unhappiness on Tom, and after what had been going on with his anger and interference, I was glad he had calmed down and accepted the decision he made.

"Yes, Tom is choosing simplicity," Alex said. "This is really cool!" Alex said with more excitement and personality than I had seen from her thus far. "Okay, let's do five cards on Jay. Choose five—no, give me seven cards," Alex said. "There is a very important message for you. Jay is saying to you, 'Will you please stop being so careful with me in this body?' He wants you to know that he's definitely in there."

Alex paused and then continued. "He's in Tom's body. He understands why you are being so careful, because it means a lot to you. So you are being very delicate. You're afraid to grab him and hold him and just go with it. Love him passionately. That's what he's saying."

"Yes, that sounds just like Jay. Okay, yes, I'll open up more." As I thought about it, I realized I was being a little apprehensive. I was always looking for clues, pieces of Jay. "I will admit although I can see, feel, and tell so much of Jay is with us, he is still a bit standoffish. It's almost like he is hesitant with that last piece of letting go and being the truly demonstrative man Jay always was." I sighed. "It is so much better than it was, though!"

"Dive in. Be passionate. Love him intensely," Alex continued. "He is saying to you, 'Be with me. Be with me. I'm here, baby. I'm with you! Cut this fear off that I am too delicate. Don't feel like you are going to lose me again.' Got it?"

"So 'Dive in, Carolyn,'" I said with a giggle. "Okay, I get it."

"Jay wants me to say to you, 'You got what you wanted. I'm back with you. You got your wish.'" Alex paused.

"That's for sure. I guess getting Jay back could be considered the epitome of manifestation, couldn't it?" I said, smiling.

"You can manifest, Carolyn. You are an earth angel, and you can manifest powerfully. Be careful of your mind-set. Keep it positive and happy," Alex said. "You need to be careful what you wish for. Be very careful. Don't manifest any earthquakes," Alex said. We both laughed.

"So here it is. It's time to let the part of your spirit that is still mourning him go. There is a part of you that hasn't let go of that mourning from the past. There is still some sadness there," Alex went on.

"Yes, well, I anticipated him to come back as a walk-in exactly the way he was when he was here before. He was an actor, creative, musical, deep, and passionate. And of course, that didn't exactly happen. But it's quite the role he is playing now," I said, giggling.

"Yes, isn't it?" Alex began. "One soul with a history with you, in the body of another man—who also has history with you. Pretty complicated role."

"Right." I laughed lightly. "That's what Jay relayed to me from the other side before the soul transference took place. 'It's complicated.' I had no idea at the time what this was all going to evolve into. But the changes in him have been amazing. He is a completely different person who looks exactly the same," I continued. "We are working through it."

Alex continued. "Jay is saying, 'See me one hundred percent. We have passionate love and a strong future together.'"

"Okay, Jay. Got it," I replied. "Our life together starts this very moment. It won't look the same as it did twenty years ago, but it is our life together. I am so grateful to have you back with me."

"What an incredible story." Alex said. Then she asked, "Any other questions?"

"Do you love what you do?" I asked Alex.

"I do," she said thoughtfully. "I'm here to show people simplicity. That material things are not the answer. When people want money, money, money, it's my job to let them know it's not money they want; it's freedom."

"I know! It never is. How did we get that way?" I replied.

"Fear. Fear of not enough," Alex said.

"Thinking we're not enough unless we have enough," I offered.

"Yep, exactly," Alex replied.

I looked at the clock and noticed we were at the end of our time. "Thank you so much, Alex. I really enjoyed meeting you, and I learned a lot." I collected my things and got up to leave.

"It was a pleasure meeting you. You are a lucky lady," Alex said.

We embraced, and I left the shop. I had a lot to think about.

51

SHARING THE JOURNEY

"Twenty cards, one at a time. Put your left hand over the deck, and say your name. You seem to have a lot of stress. It's going between your third eye and your chest, which is fascinating to me. It's almost like your third eye is creating radar in some way," April said as we began our reading. "Is Jaymie still traveling?" she asked. "I'm getting that it's not that he will have less travel; he will have more periodic travel."

"That's happening now," I said. "He's started to work from home much more. He's setting things up that way. He wants to be home as much as possible now." I was thrilled that he wanted to be home more and didn't like traveling anywhere near as much as Tom did and was trying to find a way to stay home permanently.

"Whatever you do, don't look backward. It's showing new beginnings, major changes, a lot of things happening quickly. New friends, but they are coming in with their own rules," April continued. "It shows strength through psychic friends, and you have options and choices that you haven't considered yet. It says you will have some things at a distance, and whether you will make choices at a distance… you are learning through marriage.

"Do know Jay loves you with all his heart. Bless his heart," April continued. "He's still fluctuating back and forth between the two personalities?" April asked.

"Mm-hmm," I replied. "Nowhere near as much, though. Everything has changed since we last talked, from the standpoint of logistically how life works, as well as his personality. He's home a lot more now. He wants to be with us. He works remotely as often as he can. He gets up, he makes breakfast, he makes dinner, and he takes care of Sam. And he is not doing it begrudgingly. He's happy about it—enjoying it and taking pride in it." I stopped to take a breath. "We laugh together, and everything is wonderful. It's not a hundred percent Jay. It may still be ten percent Tom," I continued. "I know he still needs to keep some of Tom's memories to do his job. But I am beginning to understand what the new normal will be for us. I like it."

"Nice," April said, smiling.

"But I tell you when the Tom part creeps up, he presses my buttons to upset me, which he is very good at. Everything changes. He yells, loses his temper, and locks himself in his office like a little child. It's awful. It's so distressing. Then two days later, it's all great again. But now it happens much less often."

We both laughed, knowing too well how Tom could press my buttons.

"Did I ever tell you that Jay came to me when he was on the spirit side one night and exclaimed, 'I'm going to be a father!'?" April said.

"No, really? That's adorable," I said. "All those years ago, I truly believed that Jay wanted no part of parenthood, and now this. That warms my heart."

"Yes, he was so happy about it and so proud to be given the opportunity," April replied.

"Well, he's good at it. That's for sure. Our house is happy, laughter all the time, and Jaymie is so much calmer, caring, and giving," I replied.

"I just know he loves you, loves you, loves you with every bone in his body," April said with emotion.

I looked at April, and sighed lightly.

"And I'm serious," April said. "Know that. Own it. I do know that he still has too many rules for himself that come from the old personality of Tom. In other words, there are some things that seem to be engrained in us, in our brains, as we are growing up. He is still having a difficult time with those things."

"He is so different now. But I do see some very specific things that haven't changed. Part of his linear personality—things have to be done his way, methodically. He has trouble just relaxing sometimes," I replied.

"Don't be surprised if he gets tickets or season tickets to some kind of shows or plays—I see you going to some kind of musical," April continued.

"Wow," I thought to myself. If there was one thing that said to me the man I was now married to was more Jay than Tom, it was that statement. "That's so nice. I have asked for tickets to live performances every Christmas for as long as I can remember. Tom always said we couldn't afford it. I knew he just didn't want to go," I explained.

"Well, I see him trying to get season tickets for you. I know he's looking into it. Okay?" April replied.

"Yes! That's wonderful!" I was so happy about this.

"Don't be surprised if he ends up on the board of some theatre group," April continued.

"Really?" I asked, not sure I could see it happening, but what a great melding of the two personalities: Jay's performing arts talent and Tom's business mind.

April went on. "You know, it's kind of like that part of him that wants to act and perform is bubbling up. And he doesn't quite know what to do with it or what it is that's happening to him." She paused. "I'm getting from my guides that he will end up being a master of ceremonies or something like that in the future."

"Yes!" I said with excitement. "That would be wonderful, and I think he would love it!"

"Okay, hold on. Tom is here now from the other side," April said. "He wants you to know that he has been through counseling. He went through his life review and didn't like what he saw. He's saying, 'I didn't realize I treated you as badly as I did.'"

I listened intently.

"He wants you to know that he's sorry he was so angry in this world. He treated you so badly because he resented everyone and everything." She paused. "He's explaining to me that he doesn't know what triggered it all. He was just in the mind-set and couldn't get himself out of it."

"You know, it's interesting," she continued, "and not uncommon to listen to someone who is raging, spouting off, and you don't understand why, or it seems there is no explanation for it. Oftentimes the person in the rage has no idea why it is happening either. He is in a mind-set and can't get himself out of it. It could be something from a past life or something buried in his subconscious that he can't put his finger on is the cause for being upset."

"That would explain a lot," I said. "In so many instances."

"Doesn't it?" April replied. "But do realize that there's nothing you or anyone else could have done to change Tom's thinking or stop the rage. He didn't know what was going on when he was here. He just resented everything."

"Makes sense. I haven't seen aspects of Tom for a long time, and I have a feeling Jaymie is on the verge of something. I think he is wondering, thinking that there is something more. One last burst, and I feel like Tommie will be completely gone," I explained.

"Could be," April said, nodding her head, deep in thought.

"Because his personality now is *awesome!*" I said joyfully.

"I just know that the psychic tie between you two is going to get much, much stronger now. It's almost like a fifth-dimensional communication between you two," April said. "That's where you are finishing each other's sentences and knowing what the other one is thinking. You'll know he's going to call before the phone rings—those types of things."

"Really?" I said. "That's great. I think I have noticed a bit of it already. I'll pay more attention."

"Good," April said, smiling. "I'm so excited for you."

April continued with the reading, looking over the cards in front of her. "Don't rush change. This shows there are big changes coming.

There is security with this change. It shows there is an offer coming out of the New York–Connecticut direction."

"Oh, this again! That message comes through every time!" I said to April. Then I thought back through other messages received, even from other mediums I was friendly with—several times something came up about the New York–Connecticut area. "I'll just have to wait and see," I thought to myself.

"This change is going to affect the family," she said. "Has your mother-in-law passed yet?" April asked, changing the subject.

"No, she's still hanging on," I answered. "She just turned ninety and is despondent when we visit her, but one of us goes at least once a week to see her."

"He's going to go through a terrible depression when that finally does happen. And I think that is going to be the final letting go for Tom. Because all Tom's pain will culminate in that. I feel it coming right out of the heart. And it's like that final burst will release him," April reported.

"That does make sense," I replied, thinking about how all this had affected Tom's spirit as well. It couldn't have been easy for him, watching Jay take over his family. I was hoping that in some way he could be released from his anguish.

"This shows communication, new beginnings. There are a lot of pieces coming together. Security, becoming aware, suppressed awareness…" April said.

"Who's suppressing? Is it me?" I asked.

"I think he is," she said. "He may start having flashbacks or memories, things that just won't make sense to him. From the Jay side of things."

"Right. Because Jay was given permission from the other side to remember his life and all this," I began. "And now we need to just let it happen in his own time. That's exciting," I replied.

"The irony is you're not going to be sure how the family is going to handle it, and he's not going to be sure that he wants to hear it,"

April said, with her "Elvis has left the building" look in her eyes. I assumed we were back on the subject of writing a book about all this.

"You're going to write the book, put the pieces together, and sit on it a little while to see his response."

"To the book or to the whole situation?" I asked.

"The whole thing," April answered. "Do you know that your releasing this book is actually going to divorce you from your own independence? Meaning, people are going to be putting their two cents into your business. You may not want to use real names. Write it like a fictional story—that's real. A fictitious real story," April said, smiling at her little joke.

"Okay, I'll have to think about that," I replied. "I'm not sure I would want to, but we'll see. I'm not looking to write it for any other reason than it may help someone become more aware of what is around them, maybe help raise their consciousness a little. Can it bring people insight? Help people understand more about the other side? I would love to open up the possibility to people that there is so much more!" I said.

"That's part of why it is so important that it's written," April added.

"To me, the story is not over until Jay becomes awake and aware. But I am getting all these messages and inspirations to get this book written. I need to start it, maybe not finish it. I don't know if the story will ever be over. I just know it has to start flowing," I responded, thinking about the bigger picture this little book was tied to.

"Right," April replied. "I just know that it can't be shelfed. But it is also not time to release it."

"I get it. I will wait until it is obvious it should be released," I said.

April began, "Remember when we had that case when I was talking to your grandmother? Wasn't it she that acted as the go-between before the transfer? Off in the distance were two guides in oatmeal-colored robes. They were talking of ascended masters and how they were exploring this way of doing things as an option to bring them onto the earth."

"I remember," I said.

"Well, they are here again, and I'm just trying to understand how they are trying to pull all these pieces together. Your story is important. It's almost like it has to play itself out to be important," she said.

"Yes. I understand. That seems like an incredibly big deal to me. I will stay the course and help however I can." The thought was overwhelming. I wouldn't have a clue as to where to begin to help. I'd just stay open and see where it all led me.

"Yes, good. A lot of this is going to come with a new determination. You can do whatever you set your mind to. You need to get it out—it may be rewritten, but you do need to start writing," April said.

"Okay," I replied.

"I find the journey you have been on with this the most fascinating thing in the world," April said with emotion.

"Me too. It is all pretty amazing," I replied. "Who knew an average Josephine like me could have such an incredible love story?"

"Carolyn, there is nothing average about you," she replied, laughing.

"Oh, I don't know. I think everyone is pretty special in their own way," I answered back. "Oh! And do you know what I realized, what inspiration came to me just a few days ago?" I said excitedly.

April looked at me with an inquisitive look. "What? Tell me."

"Well, as you know, I wanted to wait until Jaymie became fully awake and aware before I wrote this book, because that is what I thought it was supposed to look like." I felt as if I were climbing up onto my soapbox, but it was an important epiphany to me. "I've been holding back, but I keep getting inspiration and messages to start writing. And then I got it! Wham! It hit me! It doesn't matter what it looks like! It is not about what I think it needs to look like and sound like—it just needs to be truthful and authentic!" I smiled widely as I looked at April, getting my point across.

I took a breath and continued. "This is an ongoing, ever-changing story. This isn't about me; this is about an average middle-aged woman that is part of this incredible love story. And the great thing is it can happen to anyone!" I said excitedly. "It doesn't matter what you look like, where you come from, or what you do. Love is everywhere. Even if it is just a slight shifting of your heart—or an incredible story like this—everyone can have love. There is nothing to be afraid of with death—all of it is great!" I said, clapping my hands together. I was in complete joy in my revelation. "It is so clear to me. We are all connected," I continued excitedly. "Oh, I've got chills and goose bumps everywhere!"

"It's all part of the story that is happening for you..." April said.

"And really, it's only been a few years, and me being an impatient sort, I want everything to happen right away," I said as I snapped my fingers. "A few years is nothing. It's nothing! And I look back now to when you and I first started having these conversations. What an incredible journey it's already been! It's not over!"

"Right," April replied. "But the cards are telling me that you need to remember not to get defensive. Stand up for yourself, but don't get defensive. Remember codependency is over for you. Okay?"

"Yes," I agreed. "I've come so far on my own spiritual journey. The more I open up, the more I awaken, the more sense it all makes." I was through making my point. It was time for me to get off my soapbox.

"Good," April replied.

"I need to just let it unfold exactly the way it's supposed to." I looked up to the ceiling. "I'll stay out of the way and only help where needed. I promise," I said to the ether for the benefit of my spiritual guides and angels.

"My only concern with this is that people are going to wish their husbands' souls would leave and someone else would take over!" April joked. She and I both laughed heartily.

"Yes!" I said. "Can you imagine women saying to their husbands, 'You are driving me crazy. Why can't you be somebody else?'"

"Did I tell you that I talked to Patrick on the other side about this?" April said.

"No," I replied. April's husband, Patrick, had died about ten years earlier. They communicated often in spirit.

"Yes, I asked him if he wanted to come back as a walk-in," she said, smiling at me, as though she was very proud of herself.

"Did you really?" I said, giggling.

"I did!" she said, smiling.

"Well, what was his response?" I asked.

April laughed. "He said to me, 'I already died. I don't want to do that again!'"

We both laughed at the irony of it.

"But this was also not the life you were meant to live," April said, getting back on track with her thoughts. "And that is the first thing I remember Jay communicating to me at our first reading. You were not living the life you were meant to have. And that was upsetting him."

"I was so miserable, so unhappy. I still can't get over how he requested this whole thing to happen just so we could be together again. We really have such a small glimpse into how things work on the spirit side, don't we?" I said. "But we're learning."

52

SOME THINGS NEVER CHANGE

"Jay is saying that he hates the glasses and he can't understand why he doesn't know what contacts are," April said as she was communicating with Jay's spirit on the other side. "He also doesn't like the fact that he looks like an old man, but he's glad that you put up with that."

"Well, I think he is adorable," I said, smiling. "And you can tell him that."

April continued. "He wants you to know that on one level he knows everything. But on a physical level, it's harder. It seems like he's more worried about losing memories from Tom's side. He's laughing. He says, 'I lived my life on earth like a Ferrari, but I got a Ford for a body. Not much under the hood.'"

I laughed. "Yes, that sounds about right. Tom and Jay were two very different people. I see he still has his sense of humor."

"He says he's happier now," April said.

"Than he was when he first got here?" I asked. It had been about four years since the transfer happened. It was nice to know that he was happier as well.

"Than when he first got here, yes," April replied. After a short pause, she continued. "He said, 'You think it's like a soul leaves, and there is a shell, and another soul comes. But it doesn't feel that way. It doesn't come that way.' He said his system gets jammed every once in a while, and he got confused in his thinking, so he had to back up and take it slower."

This made perfect sense to me as to why the process was taking some time. It was a delicate balance he was trying to maintain.

"He says, 'Sorry for the outbursts, but you know it wasn't me,'" April said. "It's more like when you love somebody, you think before you speak and before you act. Tom never did that. Sometimes Tom's reactions take over automatically," she explained.

I looked at her and thought about some of the discussions we had, arguments even, where Jaymie would have an automatic knee-jerk reaction to something simple. He would react in the way Tom would, not the way Jay would. It was subsiding, but I was aware of what he was apologizing for.

"He wants you to know that he had a lot of the youthful thinking that you have when you die young. He's saying to me that you are not worried about making mistakes as much as you just want to get things done," April continued.

"I never thought about that. But I can see what he means," I replied.

"He's talking about Tom, that Tom has tried to talk to him several times on the other side. Jay has concerns about him. When he got the idea to make the switch, he never thought about how this was going to affect Tom. He took this on as a mission with a young man's vision, never thinking he was hurting anyone else in the process. Tom was unhappy, you were unhappy, and his passion for you drove him to make this change without thinking of the consequences to Tom. Jay had compassion for Tom and for the fact that he took over his life and his family and ultimately harmed him. He saw that Tom was really upset and resented Jay for it. But Jay understood. Jay had compassion for Tom's position, but he wasn't going to give you back," April said, smiling. "He's saying, 'It's easy to judge someone when you're not walking in their shoes.' Then with a twinkle in his eyes and says, 'But he was a bit of an ass.'"

"This is classic Jay!" I said softly, laughing.

April went on. "He did say that Tom tried to log in after the switch was made, and they had to stop him. Jay's saying, 'It's like Tom wanted both worlds at the same time. And then he just got mad at me.' He's also saying, 'It's weird to feel conscious and unconscious at the same time.' But he has been advised not to push it, because the physical mind can only handle so much," April said.

She paused for a moment. "He wants you to know that he connects to you writing this book," she said.

"Oh, I can feel that. It is absolutely flowing out of me! I must be connecting with him somehow," I replied softly, thinking about how easily the words to write came to me and that I knew I was getting help from the spirit side. "Absolutely." I giggled and said, "Especially some of the sex stuff I was writing. I knew I was getting some help there!"

We both laughed.

April continued, "He gets this kind of shit-ass grin once in a while, like he's about to say something and he's thinking about how it is going to be received..."

"Ha-ha-ha, yes!" I said. "I can picture him doing that!"

"And then he just went, 'Mmm,'" April said, laughing.

"Oh!" I exclaimed. "Absolutely, yes! That is exactly what he would have done! And did!" I paused and then continued. "Do you know that's a line I wrote in the book?"

"No, did you really?" April asked. "I just know he just got kind of this shit-ass grin and went 'Mmm.'"

"Yes, oh, that's so great!" I said excitedly.

"He's saying that he has to back up to go forward again," April continued. "They are going to try something different this time. He is kind of frustrated. He's saying, 'They can't shake me awake. I have to take it slow.' And he seems very serious about this."

April paused, deep in her spirit state. "There are two guides that just showed up. He is introducing them to me. He said, 'This one is Tom, and this one is Joe.' And they just turned around and smiled at me. They are the ones that are helping him with all this. And Jay said, 'Go figure, another Tom.'" April and I both laughed.

"Um, he keeps telling me to tell you, 'Honey, it's going to be okay. It's all going to be okay.'"

"Aww…" I said, feeling very peaceful. "I believe him."

"He says, 'Go ahead and write the book. I will take my chances with this.' Because they are working on getting it incorporated into his physical world. The knowing of this," April said. "But he's saying, 'The frustrating part of this is getting it between the conscious knowing and the unconscious knowing.'" April paused. "He's also saying, 'It's surprising how much the body lives in an unconscious state.' And then he laughs, and he says, 'I am better though!'"

We both laughed. April continued. "He just told me to tell you, 'Just pretend I'm a lollipop, and lick me all over!'"

"Oh, that's what I've missed, that sense of humor! I want him back! It was always about sex with Jay," I said, laughing joyfully.

"He said, 'Believe me. I won't fight you,'" April giggled.

"Yeah, oh, man…" I said, softly sighing. Some things never change.

"He wants to know if there is anything you need to know," April asked.

"No, I can be patient as he continues to slowly become aware of what's happening," I said. "I look forward to many years of memories and talking about how wonderful this all has been."

"He is saying there are so many pieces, so many parts to this whole thing that he's trying to figure out," April said. "He's saying the only thing that makes him sad is that he has done so much to take care of Tom's family. He said, 'I miss my family.'" She continued, "He wants you to know that some of Tom's memories were so strong that they overshadowed any memory Jay had of his own family. He's saying he did for them what he would have done for his own."

"Yeah, he really has done a lot," I said, thinking about how much Jaymie did to take care of Tom's family. The constant visits to Tom's mother in the nursing home and helping with the rental property, day in and day out. He was there to help with anything they needed. And he did it all happily.

April went on. "There is a sadness there that he ultimately can't reach out to his own family right now. He's saying, 'When I was in pure spirit, I was able to do that.' He says, 'There are notes there that talk about the sacrifices I made.'" He was referring to the piles of notes I had compiled to share this story. "'That is one of them.'"

"Oh," I said sadly. "That's a lot to give up."

"He wants you to know that's how important you are to him," April said.

I put my hand on my heart, peaceful in the love and warmth.

"He's saying that he would like to talk to you more this way, but he's saying that your mind hasn't quite caught up to the whole thing," April said.

"In what way?" I asked softly.

"What I'm doing is talking to Jay soul to soul. The soul in me reaches to the soul in him. He saying, 'But your earth mind takes over, and you second-guess what you are hearing,'" April reported.

"Yes, all right. I'll work on it." I admitted I was having trouble deciphering messages I was receiving, and I really wanted to communicate this way. I would work on improving.

April continued. "But he wants you to be patient with yourself. It's not a command or a demand. It's just something you can work on."

"Okay," I said. "Can I ask, is he going to be able to see his family? Oh, it breaks my heart what he has given up."

"He isn't sure yet. He says, 'Honey, only time can tell that. But we don't need both of us to worry about this, because it is not helping anyone. It's just a piece of my heart that gets lost sometimes,'" April said.

"Okay," I said softly.

April asked, "Is there anything you want to ask him at this point?"

"Is he happy?" I asked.

"He says, 'My heart is happy. In every life there are losses and gains, and you just have to take them as they come.' He says, 'I'm no Dalai Lama, but I've learned a lot.'"

I was touched and overwhelmed with everything that was happening, and tears welled up in my eyes. "I just want him to know how much I appreciate what he has done for me. And just how much things have changed and my life is so much better," I said through tears. "Which I know was his point."

"He said, '*Our* life—it's our life together. Try to remember that,'" April reported.

"Yes, of course," I said softly. I thought about how incredible and interesting the years to come would be with this man in my life. The journey so far had been fascinating and fun, and sometimes overwhelming and frustrating, but it was getting better as each day passed.

"Okay, I have a question," I started. "When he becomes awake finally, do I get my old Jay back?" I was so grateful for how far we had come, but this part of Jay—this way of communicating with him—was so pure, so real, it was 100 percent Jay. What I shared everyday with Jaymie was great and consistently getting better, but I missed this.

"He's saying that as far as he understands, there is an incorporation between who he was and who he is now. And that ultimately there are a lot of things that you remember about him from years ago, and some of them were not important enough for you to hold on to. He says to beware of memories and expectations. 'We have to form this together,' he said. 'Please remember I have taken on a lot to try to accomplish this,'" April explained.

"Yes, of course. I don't mean the memories as much as I mean the personality of Jay, the soul of Jay, the spirit of him. So much is here now that there is no doubt he's back with me," I explained.

"You have to remember it's only been three years in this whole process. The more relaxed he is in the day-to-day stuff, the more that part of him will incorporate," April said. "It will make it easier for him."

"Okay, and he is very relaxed now, and I do notice much more of Jay's personality emerging," I said happily.

"And he is very funny!" April said. "He is very flip." We both laughed, thinking about some of the things he had said to us.

"He just wants you to know how much he loves you and how much it is not a sacrifice to do this with you," April said, eyes searching. "But there are pieces he knows that still have to happen. He's not sure how it plays out. He wants you to know he's on a wait-and-see method too. He says, 'I think you know I'm getting bolder as time goes on.'"

"Yes, I do," I said softly. "And funnier, and happier, and calmer, and all of it."

"From what I'm understanding from Joe and Tom—his guides for this transfer—part of this has to do with the incorporation and getting back to the idea that in order to hold on to Tom's knowledge for his job, they couldn't wipe those memories out. So it's not like Tom's memories got replaced. They had to be incorporated."

"With Jay's," I said. "They need to be slowly incorporated with Jay's memories."

"Yes," April replied. "Remember his earth mind couldn't take this all at once. He's talking about the guides that are watching over him and this transfer, the process of it all. They seem really pleased with what's happening. They seem to feel that he's pretty much on target for what they expected, or what they could imagine would happen. He's doing extremely well. This is going extremely well," April reported.

"That's because he's awesome!" I said softly, forever Jay's cheerleader.

"But you need to know that three years is not much at all in their time," April said.

"I...I do know that. There really is no time on the spirit side," I replied.

"But you've got to remember that this is the rest of your life. And that he's happy to share the rest of your life with you. And he's happy he is going to motivate himself to do more, move forward more," April continued.

"And this book won't disrupt him?" I asked. "I just don't want it to mess anything up." I felt torn between getting this story out to people and keeping it all to ourselves, in a safe little cocoon.

"He said go ahead," April reported. "He'll take his chances with it."

"Take his chances with it?" I asked. "So what does that mean? I wonder...I just don't want it to jeopardize how far he has come..."

"Meaning, he doesn't know for sure how the book is going to incorporate into his physical world yet, but he does know that it's important that it is written. And it's necessary. Think of it like this: you bringing his subconscious mind along in the spiritual journey you are on is going to be key in kicking in his higher centers," April explained. "So that the real Jay can stand up, he's telling me."

"So just do it. Let it flow," I replied.

"Right," April said. "It will either bring him to an awakening state, or he will fall into Tom's old memories. He cannot guarantee at this point which way it will go, but he'll take his chances. He knows it is important that it is released," April said.

"Okay, so as I continue on my spiritual journey, sharing all this with him—slowly and in pieces, I would think—is going to be key in kicking in his higher spiritual centers," I said, explaining it to myself so I would fully understand. "So do it. Let it flow..."

"He wants you to know that 'as funny as I was, and as open minded as I could be, a lot of this stuff is a lot for me to handle too.'"

"I can imagine," I replied.

"I'm asking questions now..." April said.

"Yes, of course, April. Go for it!" I replied.

"I am asking him how he thought to do this," April started. "He's saying that when he found out he could do this...'There are councils over here. We have guides and other people...'"

April paused. "Jay is explaining to me, 'I was beside myself watching what was going on with you, watching what was happening with you, and I just couldn't take it anymore, so I started asking questions. How can this be changed? How can she have a better life? How can this be different?'" April paused. "And then he said to someone, 'This was not the life she was meant to have. If I was there instead of Tom, she would have a better life.'" April paused again. "And they said to me, 'Why don't you find out if you can do that?' And I said, 'Well, what the hell, I will!' And that's how he said it all started," April said.

April and I looked at each other and burst out in jubilant laughter. For years, we had wondered how all this took place, how he could do this, and why it seemed to be such an important thing on the spirit side, not just in our little world. And there it was, simple as could be.

"Oh, wow, that's amazing!" I said. "And then from there, he was a man on a mission."

April chuckled and said, "He just said, 'You know when I'm on a mission!'"

"Wow," I said softly. "Yes, I do know what he's like when he's on a mission!" I thought happily. "Very persistent!"

"From everything they just told me, everything I saw, and everything they are explaining to me...if they had come in and just made the switch from Tom to Jay, you would have Jay back, but then there would have been a lot of other chaos. It would have been more chaotic for the kids, and for you, so it was judged that the whole family would suffer if they made the complete switch at one time."

"Sure," I said. "I see." It did make sense to me.

"All right?" April asked, making sure I understood.

I nodded.

"So as the negotiations came between Tom and Jay, Jay understood that he would have to sacrifice some of his memory of self in order to take on the responsibilities that Tom had." April paused. "Which meant Jay relying more on Tom's body's biological knowledge and intellectual knowledge. It wasn't like Tom trained him for the job." April chuckled. "So he had to tap in completely to Tom's knowledge in order to continue doing that job. But it was the only way he could think of to provide for you and the family in the condition that he thought you should have someone take care of you."

"I understood why he did it. That seems like quite a sacrifice right there. Jay's heart is creative and in the performing arts, not business," I said, realizing how much Jay had done and given up for us to be together again. My heart was ready to burst.

"Remember it was Jay's choice," April reminded me. She knew I was feeling sad that Jay was doing a job he did not love, to take care of us.

"Okay, I will try not to worry about what he gave up, because he said not to..." I said lightly, for my benefit more than April's. "And besides, our new life is just beginning..."

Both April and I sat in silence for a few moments, letting the enormity of it all sink in.

April continued. "And they are still trying to understand it all on the spirit side, trying to make sense out of it, logic out of it. It is a new process that we are all muddling through. They are also trying to work through everything that's happening, how it's happening, the way it's happening, and what works and what doesn't work."

"So we're in great company," I said.

"One of Jay's guides just asked me to tell you not to worry about the other mediums, because they have never experienced this. How are they supposed to know?" April reported.

"Yes, of course, they wouldn't have any of the background," I said. I had seen a few mediums. Some had picked up on what was happening in my world and understood it, a couple were just plain curious but didn't really understand, and a couple of others told me it just wasn't true. I decided the best thing I could do to honor this incredible journey I was on was to listen to my instincts, my intuition, and what I knew in my heart. Everyone else could go pound sand as far as I was concerned.

"The spirit world doesn't have the background to understand it either, which is why they are being so careful with everything," April added. "You're a test case."

I laughed.

April said, laughing, "I have to tell you this. Jay just said to me, 'No, she's a head case.'"

"Oh, yeah?" I said, laughing.

"I gotta say this because it's funny: he's going like this with his eyebrows." She looked at me and did a little Groucho Marx eyebrow move, lifting them up and down.

"Oh, that kind of head?" I asked. "Of course." We both laughed. "That is exactly what popped into my mind as soon as you said it, but I decided not to mention it because it seemed too dirty minded!"

We both laughed.

"You know, the bottom line is that he wants you to know he loves you," April said. "He's saying, 'Whatever we have to go through, as long as we have a good life and we're happy, I don't care what else happens. I want you to know that's the truth.'"

Tears welled in my eyes. "This incredible love. Just let him know how much I appreciate everything he has done to bring us back together and how much I love him right back."

April said, "He knows."

THE JOURNEY GOES ON

Here is where I end this part of my story.

Thank you for allowing me to share it with you. After years of researching, picking apart, and analyzing, with both belief and skepticism, I have been convinced that something very special has happened as my life and my story unfold. During this, a few facts have become obvious to me. First, I am one very fortunate human being, who is truly grateful for her life. Second, I have been given a beautiful gift from the love of my life. And third, this could happen to anyone. There is nothing special about me, nothing out of the ordinary or different. I am just another soul wandering around the earth, trying to make it through each day with a little grace and dignity.

I can come up with lots of things that have changed about my husband in an effort to prove that this transfer has taken place, to both you and myself. But the fact is that he has changed, and I can see the difference. A difference in the way he looks at me, a difference in the way he talks to me. A difference in how we just love to be around each other. It's easy, it's simple, and it's real. The soul connection is back.

Day by day, Jay becomes more aware. His personality, actions, conversations, outlook, thought patterns, and sense of humor become stronger. The changes are no longer subtle, they are blatant, and many times I can only shake my head and give him a hug, which these days he accepts enthusiastically.

I am grateful for what has been given to me. I am grateful for the incredible love I share with this man who has moved heaven and earth to make a better life for me, for us. Now I can be myself again with him by my side. My true, authentic self, sturdy legs and all.

As I end this part of the story, I realize it is just the beginning of our new life story. There is so much more to come. I'll keep you posted.

Life is good again.

Carolyn

A MESSAGE FROM APRIL

Words - just seven simple words "Do You Know What a Walk-in is?" changed my world forever. Now you wouldn't think that seven words could do so much, but they did! The day I met Carolyn for her first reading started out like any other day. I would quickly find out that the journey on which we were about to embark was far from ordinary. Intense and enlightening are the words that keep coming to mind.

Before Carolyn sat down, with her flashing beautiful smile, Jay's spirit was before me, bigger than life and with a personality to match. Communicating with spirits for the past 40 years, I have seen, heard and learned quite a bit about the spirit world and how they live. The likes of Carolyn's reading was not something I was prepared for. I was most taken with the sheer intensity with which Jay communicated with me. He had determination, passion and intense concern for the woman that he kept saying was the great love of his life. He brought through our communication his desire to make her life better with emotions that were far beyond anything I know how to express with simple words. This was like nothing I have ever experienced before in a reading.

As he repeated over and over "this is not the life she signed up for, it's not the life she agreed to," his angst and frustration was palpable. He was beside himself that Carolyn was not living the life she deserved. He was frustrated and angry as he watched over her from the spirit side, and he was completely determined to change her circumstances and come back to her. Jay seemed prepared to take on the universe to do it.

My job as a medium is to repeat what I am being told from the spirit side, exactly as I hear it, without judgement or insertion of my own perspective. Because of my experience, I can tell when someone is being honest with me, and when someone is not. During this first reading, every bone in my body knew this was true and authentic. I was overwhelmed with the love and genuineness Jay shared with me. I knew instantly that this was something far more reaching than anything I had come across before. I also knew this was important, and I knew this was special.

I must admit, at any other given time, I may not have believed this soul transfer could actually take place, or that walk-ins were real. I may not have believed the walk-in phenomenon, had it not been presented to me several times just prior to this first reading with Carolyn.

I have been given proof along the way through spirit connections that settled the truthfulness of what was happening in my own mind. I believe Carolyn and Jay's reading was presented to me through divine synchronicity. Having the knowledge of communication allowed me to be prepared and guide Carolyn through this process from the earth-bound side, as spirits answered her questions, concerns, and discussed it all with her in detail.

As we have learned through our spirit guides, Carolyn and Jay would have married later in their lives. The fact that Jay died before his time was something he was also struggling with on the other side. I believe if his conscious earth mind had known they would have been together after all, or had kept the hope alive that Carolyn would come back to him, he would have survived the surgery. In this case, Carolyn and Jay would have gotten together and lived the life they were meant to live, and accomplished the things they were supposed to in this lifetime. Jay has let me know on a few occasions that he died of a broken heart, thinking he lost her forever.

You may have wondered why the spirit world has given permission for Jay to do this, as we were told this type of walk-in has never been done before in this way. We still don't know for sure. From his simple request to come back, through permissions, contracts and negotiations, we are learning more and more about the spirit world, the inner workings, and just how logical, orderly, and incredible it all is.

What is fascinating to me as a medium, and something I believe is so rare, is that the guides, angels, and Grand Council have opened up to us and shared their thoughts, opinions, plans, and reactions about this love story, and how it would all play out. They have guided us with respect and humor throughout the process. Because of this, we understand intimate details about the soul transfer process. We have also learned how some decisions are made, and an idea of how things develop on the spirit side. The glimpse into the greater universe we have been privy to is something I will always cherish.

Other than their own personal guides, which we all have with us, Jay and Carolyn both have specific guides to work with them on this transfer progression, and to support them through their personal awakening process. From what we can understand, it should be quite an incredible life ahead for them, finally together again. I'm very happy for them, after everything they have done and been through, they deserve it.

Since this journey began, I have seen the transformation from Tom to Jay. He is light hearted, demonstrative, kind, and his love for Carolyn is profound. He was given permission to remember his path from the spirit side and I look forward to one day soon when Carolyn, Jay and I can all sit back in front of a roaring fire and laugh, cry, and share our thoughts on this incredible journey.

One of the most important points I hope readers take from this book is not only that there really is the capacity for incredible love in this world, but that we are not alone. Ever. Our spirits, guides and angels are with us always. The universe is not a place of judgement and executioners. It is logical and intelligent, but also filled with authentic love, humor, synchronicity, and natural law. I have personally experienced that life on the other side in many ways is like life here, but on the other side souls always say they are "home". We are here on the earth to learn about ourselves in a way separate from everyone else, to learn what works and what doesn't. People often want to think it is better on the spirit side than the earth side, but in truth our own awareness governs the conditions we exist in both places.

First and foremost, this is a love story like no other. I feel privileged to be exposed to Carolyn and Jay's journey. The story of a man who loved a woman so much that he moved heaven and earth to be with her and to make her happy. He is living proof that love never, ever dies, and those who love us that have passed on, are still watching out for us, and care.

Love and peace,
April Sheerin

RANDOM THOUGHTS FROM MY JOURNAL

I wish I could say that I was a fastidious and highly organized person who has a neat journal in perfect chronological order, but I cannot. In typical Carolyn style, I collected notes with information jotted down on bits of paper, the backs of receipts, and all other manner of items that could be written on. These were then put in a large envelope for safekeeping.

They may not be perfect, but they are from the heart and reflect how I felt at the very moment I could find a pen.

July 29, 2013
This morning Sam woke up crying. "I want my daddy back," he said to me. I asked him what he meant. He just said he was sad and missed his daddy. I can't help thinking that on some level he is grieving, knows what happened. He said he had a dream where everyone was in a big room and all the kids were with their parents. Sam didn't have his dad there. Something must have hit him. I wonder.

July 29, 2013
Today Jaymie was rubbing his upper arms and chest and was complaining about a pain and soreness. He said he was just achy. I wonder if that has anything to do with the transfer.

September 3, 2013
What an interesting weekend. It was Tom's birthday, and we had planned to celebrate it with a trip to Boston and have lunch before I had to drop him off at Logan Airport. He woke me up and said that he didn't want to go. He said it didn't feel like his birthday. He was very sad. The entire day was a bust, and we had planned a wonderful day. Jaymie was overcome with sadness, saying that it just didn't feel like it was his birthday. I guess it really wasn't.

I'm trying hard to be patient, as instructed by my guides, and I am looking hard to find little signs that things are changing. So far it has so much to do with how happy and content he is. He's kind. He's calm and doesn't seem to despise me anymore. I'll take that for now!

It was a tough day. When I was in the shower this morning, the thought came to me: "I am finally loved." It was a wonderful feeling, one I haven't felt—well, have never felt before. Then it quickly changed to grief, and I started sobbing. It was a kind of release; emotions came pouring out, and I stood in the shower sobbing for a good long time. It was a grieving like I have never experienced. Maybe I was grieving for Tom, for the final betrayal of his wanting to get away from me, for the life, for the wasted years of unhappiness, false emotion, and pretending.

≈

Today, as we were getting ready to go out for the day, Sam went up to Jaymie and mussed up his hair with both hands, creating an Einstein look. It was adorable, and Jaymie didn't seem to mind one bit. Tom would have screamed at Sam for this; he never would let anyone touch his hair before. He had so much stuff in it I called him shellac man. But today he just laughed and didn't care what he looked like. Very cool.

≈

Today we were shopping for a few things we needed, and Jaymie needed to pick up some deodorant. Tom always used a specific brand that he had bought since I met him. Today Jaymie picked up a different kind and purchased it. I could swear it is the kind Jay used to use years ago. Hmmm…

≈

This weekend Jaymie went to San Francisco to see his brother and the America's Cup races. He usually loved to visit the West Coast, but this trip he was not happy. He said he didn't feel like himself and didn't enjoy the family like he usually did, almost like he didn't belong.

≈

April called today and said to me that her guides want me to know everything is fine and that I need to be patient, be a friend, not push, and believe it is all working out as it should. Perfect timing, because I have been wondering if I will see any big changes and getting a little impatient. I need to get out of my mind that Tom left, Jay came, and everything will be back the way it was when we were younger. That's not how it will happen, I'm sure. It doesn't make sense. I would love that, though! Lots of little pieces are adding up to a very wonderful Jaymie.

ॐ

I can't believe what happened today. We were in the car with Molly (our dog), and we stopped at the gas station. Molly has a mind of her own, which is one of the things Tommie couldn't stand about her, that and the fact she was "just a stupid dog."

As Jaymie stepped out of the car at the gas station, Molly slipped out of the back seat and darted into traffic. Jaymie jumped out of the car and was running around in circles after her at the intersection. There were cars screeching and honking, stopped at all points of the intersection, and Jaymie almost was hit by a car himself! He finally caught her and ran back to the car. He put her in the back seat, and we drove away.

I told him he was my hero, and he just laughed and said, "I didn't want to have to tell Sam his dog was a pancake."

ॐ

Why does it seem that Jaymie no longer has a problem hearing out of his left ear? He seems to be able to hear me and everyone else just fine. There are no more excuses, "You didn't tell me that!" when I remind him of something I said or he said.

ॐ

I cannot get over the fact that Jaymie seems to want to do anything to please me or help me. We were sitting watching a bit of TV, and

I said, "Oops, I forgot to turn off the oven." I started to get up, but he beat me to it, and he immediately got up out of his seat, went over, and turned it off for me. While he was in the kitchen, he asked if I wanted anything to drink. So simple, so sweet, yet so different.

Okay, so now Jaymie seems to love the dogs. They sit on his lap, and he plays with them, feeds them, and gives them treats. It's nice.

Jaymie surprised me with tickets to the Broadway Series at PPAC. One of them was *Pippin*, a show that includes the song "Magic to Do," which Jay used to sing to me when we were younger. A coincidence. Can't be, no such thing.

It occurred to me today—hit me like a ton of bricks actually—that I have been living my life as someone else. Anyone else. Trying to be whoever I needed to be to be loved and accepted. For my mother, for Tommie, for friends, for coworkers. I was a chameleon—I would be whoever and act however to fit in. This is how I thought I would be accepted and loved. I just wanted to be part of something, someone who was connected to others. Those actions brought me nowhere near the truth, or my authentic self. I think I may have just found her.

Lately I have been feeling like I can be me, the authentic me, and be safe in that feeling. My mother is no longer here to mess with my head, and Tommie is no longer here to judge. Jaymie is allowing this space for me to be who I am, and still loves me—blemishes, craziness, imperfections, and all. I am so grateful to him and every other soul that allowed and helped this to happen. As I have come to find out, we are all connected, every one of us…and it is a bigger and better family than I could have imagined!

Our conversations every evening while Jaymie is traveling have changed. They are shorter, sweeter, and happy. No pressure to say the right thing and report on the day with details so I can be judged. He seems to just want to touch base, say hello, and see how I am. He trusts me and knows I will take care of everything, as I always have.

Jaymie sat down next to me on the couch and put his arm around me. So simple but means so very much. He actually wants to be near me. That hasn't happened in years and years. I am falling in love with him all over again. His kindness, his calmness, his acceptance, and his affection are wonderful. I feel like a little kid, excited for what's under the Christmas tree!

Jaymie said to me today, "It is my job to take care of you. You're a ricochet rabbit." He seems proud that his job is to take care of me. I'm not sure how he figures I'm a ricochet rabbit—maybe because I get an idea in my mind and I'm off and running to make it happen, until the next one comes and I am off in another direction. He really is my rock.

Jaymie doesn't seem to worry about money at all. He is generous with money and his time. Doesn't seem to be a cheapskate anymore. We always have plenty of money; it comes easily when you don't worry about it. No more poverty consciousness. Living from abundance brings abundance.

Jaymie and I were talking about cars while I was driving him to Logan Airport to catch a flight after a long holiday weekend. I mentioned that I was thinking about a new one that was a little bigger because Sam is now taller than I am and he was uncomfortable in the back seat. "Why don't you get a Ford?" he said, joking with me. I thought back on the comment he made while in spirit about his Ferrari life going into a Ford body.

This morning, as we lay in bed talking, he leaned over and bopped me on the nose lightly with his index finger, just like he used to do when we were together years ago.

Jaymie is going to see my mother-in-law every week. He seems to be taking on his promise to Tom—his negotiations with him, anyway—with gusto. He is helping the family all the time and being very good about it. He's getting along better with the family than Tom used to. They keep asking me, "What happened to Tom? He's so happy."

He is talking with total strangers. He is kind to them, holds the door, and engages in conversation; he just seems so much happier all the time. I love this man so much. I can't believe everything he has given up to be with me. I am so blessed.

Sam and Jaymie had an argument today—and immediately Jaymie started screaming, Tom's usual knee-jerk reaction. I asked him to stop and calm down. I asked quietly. Jaymie stopped dead in his tracks and looked at me, and there seemed to be a little bit of recognition in his eyes, and he immediately calmed down. Then he and Sam talked it through. Very cool.

I don't know if I am grasping at straws here, but this weekend, while Jaymie was home, we went to the movies, and I didn't have to talk him into it. We saw a kids' movie, and he laughed out loud at some of the jokes, and I think he actually enjoyed it. Afterward he wanted to talk about it! Amazing.

I no longer feel as though I have to walk on eggshells!

Jaymie is just happier. He is so easy to have a conversation with. There are no hidden meanings, negativity, or manipulation in talking with him. He is stronger, more confident.

I haven't heard or seen Jaymie lash out or scream at any of us in a very long time. He is so much easier to have a conversation with and doesn't try to pick a fight with me to make himself "right" anymore.

Got a call from April today. She said that through her spiritual connections, she had been assigned a guide to help with the situation we were going through. It is one of the same guides that helped with the transfer process, I understand. We talked for a while. I was telling her that Jaymie and I had an argument, and she told me to just walk away, not fight back and reward the behavior—fighting back will only strengthen the behavior. She reminded me that Jay—Jaymie—doesn't know what normal is anymore. He has Jay's soul with Tom's memories. That can't be easy. I need to be patient. I can be and will do so gratefully for everything Jay has done to be back with me. This is all so incredible!

Jay is definitely coming around, slowly but surely. He has completely different reactions and responses than Tom did. We even had a few laughs about June Cleaver beads. He is so much more engaged in life and in his friends—which he now has many more of. He's straightforward, saying what he means. I love that! That I can work with. Jaymie's responses are not what I expect to come out of Tom's body—which means change.

I have been looking for hit-me-over-the-head-with-a-brick changes in Jaymie, but it is not as obvious as that. It's coming slowly, and as I think about the subtle changes and put them together, it is showing me one very different husband. I'm falling in love all over again!

⚘

This is all so fascinating and wonderful! I am so grateful that Jay has done all this to be together with me again. I'm learning more, understanding the process in our particular case more, and loving every minute of this craziness.

⚘

I will be his friend as instructed and let it all unfold. I do think Jay is much more prevalent in Tom these past few days.

⚘

Today I felt this freedom, freedom to be myself, to be who I am. This is the most amazing feeling. I realize now (and realized while it was happening too, I think) that I was trying to mold myself into someone different to please Tom—which was never going to happen. I see now that in the past I changed my humor, my personality, and how I would normally do things to keep the peace. I think it might have caused my depression in my thirties.

Now I just feel loved. It's all so perfect.

⚘

This morning I woke up with some real clarity. Jay is definitely with me. One of the most wonderful things I am feeling is that I am finally good enough. Good enough to simply be loved. Who knew the love of a wonderful partner could have that effect on you?

With Jay I can just be me. No judging.

✑

April mentioned to me on the phone today that Jay's not perfect. He's a human being too! I realize that, but he is perfect for me, so that's all that matters.

✑

This evening I reached out to Jaymie, and we made love. It was nice. I asked him afterward, "What do you think has gotten into us after so long?" I was also talking about how well we were getting along. He said, "We're both just shifting." I wonder what he is really feeling and thinking about all this.

✑

Today at lunch Jaymie made some mean comment to me—in jest— one of those "I'm only kidding but still want to get my point across" comments. Tristan called him on it. He felt bad and apologized right away. I think he was sad he said it. It was done, and we moved on.

✑

I've had the opportunity to learn a great lesson about money. Stop chasing it, and it will come. Respect it. Give it. Let it flow. If you have the true belief that money will always be there, it will.

✑

Tonight Jaymie, Sam, and I all snuggled in bed together. We read "I'm Going on a Bear Hunt" and acted out the parts, laughing and having fun. Then Jaymie started singing a children's song to Sam. He sounded pretty good!

As weeks and months move on, I see so little of Tom's personality and a much happier Jay. While we were out to dinner with the family this weekend, Jaymie did not seem to have any problem hearing, even in a noisy restaurant. He also doesn't seem to have as much trouble pronouncing some words as he had in the past. He's engaged in the group as well, not just sitting on the sidelines observing, like he used to.

This past weekend I caught Jaymie looking at me very intently. It felt like he was looking into my soul almost. I wonder what is going through his mind.

Yesterday was such a great day! Jaymie and I laughed, had long meaningful conversations, made love, played cards, and just played at life together. I feel so comfortable with him. Jay is definitely becoming more seated into Tom's body. I love this man so much!

Sam has never been happier. Tristan is so content as well; they love their new dad so much. Sam made a silly little bracelet out of rubber bands and gave it to Jaymie, who immediately put it on and wore it to work the next day. Adorable.

The toilet seat. That dreaded toilet seat. Jay and I used to have silly little arguments about his leaving the toilet seat up. It was all in good fun. He used to say, "I'm a man living alone. What difference does it make?" When I was married to Tom, he never left the seat up, probably because he lived with three women growing up and had learned it wasn't worth the effort of arguing. Now Jaymie leaves the toilet seat up all the time. It's funny to me every time I see it.

Life seems so easy now. I don't seem to be fighting with myself in my own mind anymore. When I consciously decided to let go and let God, life got so much better. By my not pushing anymore but letting the universe unfold, life has become sweet, and my relationship with my wonderful new husband and the kids is much more harmonious. I am so grateful for everything that has happened. I feel like I may actually be becoming who I was meant to be. For that I thank Jay, my guides, and God.

I have noticed that Jaymie is much healthier. He is eating better; his tastes seem to have changed as well. He has tons of energy, and he seems younger somehow…and his complexion is great. He seems to be glowing. He's finally eating more than Saugy hotdogs!

While we were seated, getting ready for the curtain to go up for the musical at PPAC, I couldn't help but think back on how many times I asked for this for Christmas with Tom, who never wanted to go and always had an excuse. A few months after the transfer, and here we are, with season tickets, completely enjoying an entire Broadway musical series. They were a gift.

🌀

"Get the hell away from me" was the way Tom greeted the dog when he came home from being on the road. Lately he is happy to see her, petting her and saying, "Molly, how the hell are you? Good to see you!" Incredible.

🌀

There seems to be less and less of Tom around—although Jaymie is getting a bit confused about things that came naturally to him before, and he's a little forgetful too. It's okay; I've got his back!

🌀

I had a dream last night:

"Jay wrote a letter to me, didn't want to say good-bye—do you know how much I love you? April came to his house, noticed things with the name Carolyn on them, toys and old 45 rpm records. Sam was introduced to Jay's friends; they all loved him. We all walked away together. Jay, April, and Sam were in one car going home; I got into another car and got lost. Couldn't find the highway, bumpy ride."

I wonder what that was all about.

🌀

Tristan said to me last night, when I was complaining about someone who had lashed out at me when I stood up for myself and was wondering how to handle the situation:

"Sometimes the best decision is no decision at all."

He said he read it in *War and Peace,* or something like that. A sign to me to give it up to the universe!

As I think more about all this, I realize I thought it was as simple as Tom out, Jay in, or at least wanted that to happen. That was definitely wishful thinking on my part, and as the months passed, I realized how perfectly structured this whole process was. Had it been a simple case of switching Jay's soul into Tom's body with an immediate transfer, fully seated, how would that have affected the kids? Our family? His position in his work—which he was so dedicated to keeping? How could that happen without raising all kinds of havoc for everyone and everything? This is not what Jay would want.

It is slow, methodical process, but each day it becomes more and more apparent that Jay is with me. The synchronicities, the coincidences, the terms and words he uses, even the tone of his voice—all Jay. There are almost none of the personality traits of Tom left. Now all that's left is for Jay to wake up to the situation that happened and be here with us fully, completely.

I was playing music in the kitchen while I was cooking. Jaymie came in and started whistling—and asked me to turn it up. He said he liked my playlist.

Jaymie was home for a week from work and got up every morning to make breakfast, he took Sam to school, planned and cooked dinner, and asked me if I needed anything a couple of times a day. What a difference!

We were watching *It's a Wonderful Life,* which is now a tradition on Christmas Day in our family, after gifts have been opened and brunch served. Later that day we watched *White Christmas*—Jaymie started singing with the movie. It was adorable. He certainly can't sing like he used to, but at least his love of music is coming back.

Jaymie is starting to ask questions about spirituality. He is interested in what I have to say about it, much more than ever before. We joke about when he will come over to "the light side." His awakening is happening, and soon, he will be fully seated into Tom's body, and we can pick up where we left off. I can't wait.

CONNECTING

Carolyn Jaymes
CarolynJaymesAuthor@gmail.com
www.ALifeByRequest.com
Facebook: www.facebook.com/carolynjaymes
Twitter: www.twitter.com/holisticonline
Pinterest: www.pinterest.com/holisticcampus/
Instagram: www.instagram.com/holisticcampus/

ABOUT THE AUTHOR

 Carolyn Jaymes is an award-winning entrepreneur and a reluctant author. An expert in marketing and business communications, she has worked with presidential candidates, celebrities, and national nonprofit organizations. Shortly after starting her own epicurean catering business in the early eighties, she was nationally recognized for the success and quick growth of her business. Jaymes has been featured in *Fast Company*, the *Boston Globe*, and several other publications as well as television and radio appearances. *A Life by Request* is her first book.